At Home in Buenos Aires

At Home in Buenos Aires

TEXT BY Edward Shaw

PHOTOGRAPHS BY Reto Guntli

Abbeville Press   Publishers

New York   London

JACKET FRONT *Nostalgia pervades the patio of Teresa Anchorena's home, providing a fitting climate for an introduction to Buenos Aires.*

JACKET BACK *Buenos Aires is a city of contrasts. Often bleak, it can be exuberantly colorful when least expected.*

PAGE 2 *A massive door opens onto the beautifully tiled entry hall of an estancia home.*

PAGE 3 *This arched doorway opening onto a balcony is typical of turn-of-the-century homes in the city.*

PAGES 4–5 *The downtown airport, as seen from the pier of the Fishing Club.*

PAGE 7 *Clockwise from top left: In the midst of a match at the Argentine Polo Grounds (see also page 81); Monuments presented by national communities or built to honor the heroic deeds of Argentina's leaders dot the city; A passion for bullfighting provides the decorative theme for this room in an estancia near Buenos Aires (see also page 190); A guitarist evokes memories of legendary tango singer Carlos Gardel; Porteños are avid collectors, often of colonial religious art from Peru and Bolivia.*

EDITOR: Jacqueline Decter
DESIGNER: Molly Shields
ART DIRECTOR: Patricia Fabricant
PRODUCTION MANAGER: Louise Kurtz

Text copyright © 1999 Ediciones Larivière. Photographs copyright © 1999 Reto Guntli. Compilation—including selection of text and images—copyright © Abbeville Press.

First edition

10 9 8 7 6 5 4 3 2 1

Map by Sophie Kittredge
Photographs on pages 24, 46 (bottom), 80, 83, 98–99 © Yann Arthus-Bertrand
Photographs on pages 108, 123, 199 © Xavier A. Verstraeten

Library of Congress Cataloging-in-Publication Data
Shaw, Edward
    At home in Buenos Aires / text by Edward Shaw ; photographs by Reto Guntli.
        p.   cm.
    Includes index.
    ISBN 0-7892-0251-4
    1. Buenos Aires (Argentina)—Description and travel. 2. Buenos Aires (Argentina)—Pictorial works.   I. Guntli, Reto. II. Title.
    F3001.S43 1999
    982'.11—dc21
99-18487

To suburbs
and Tigre

N

*Palermo
Park*

*Jorge Newbery
Airport*

Hippodrome

*Polo
Grounds*

• *Fishing
Club*

R I V E R   P L A T E

Port of Buenos Aires

PALERMO

Zoo

PALERMO
CHICO

PALERMO
VIEJO

*Botonical
Gardens*

AVENIDA LAS HERAS

AVENIDA DEL LIBERTADOR

*Recoleta
Cemetery*

RECOLETA

AVENIDA CALLAO

*Jockey
Club*

Retiro Station

B A R R I O   N O R T E

Plaza San Martín

• *Kavanagh Building*

RETIRO

• *Yacht Club*

AVENIDA SANTA FE

AVENIDA CÓRDOBA

Colón Theater •

• *Obelisk*

AVENIDA CORRIENTES

AVENIDA 9 DE JULIO

*Palacio
Barolo*

*Casa
Rosada*

PUERTO MADERO

AVENIDA INT. O. M. NOEL (Avenida Costanera Sur)

*Ecological
Reserve*

AVENIDA DE MAYO

*Congress
Building*

Plaza of the
Congress

Cabildo •

Plaza
de Mayo

AVENIDA BELGRANO

AVENIDA INDEPENDENCIA

SAN TELMO

Plaza Dorrego •

AVENIDA SAN JUAN

AUTOPISTA 25 DE MAYO

CONSTITUCÍON

LA BOCA

0   1   MI

0   1   2   KM

• *Bombonera*
(Boca Juniors
Soccer Stadium)

Contents

Introduction

Any attempt to condense life in a major city into sequences of words is doomed to reflect the writer's bias and prejudice. I have spent forty years trying to flesh out my personal portrait of Buenos Aires, both in writing and in photographs, ever since I first sailed into the basin of the River Plate on a brief visit as a college student in 1957.

This is a book of photographs that reflects the vision of a European with a highly developed sensitivity who captures, in a city hidden in the shadows of its past, a slightly out-of-focus rerun of Europe in one of the most remote corners of the globe. Photographer Reto Guntli succumbs to the shopworn charm of the city and makes no effort to disguise the flaws. His photographs record many of the facets of Buenos Aires's magnificent past, often bathed in the aura of a nostalgia that pervades both the city and its inhabitants. He takes advantage of the city's special light, which at dawn and dusk attenuates the jarring midday glare. The resolution is a clever one. Buenos Aires is not Rio de Janeiro. There is an intrinsic drabness to it that is tempered by the golden rays of the setting sun.

During its relatively brief history, Buenos Aires has intrigued foreign visitors—especially the British, who were so involved

Cupolas are a distinctive feature of the Buenos Aires skyline. Here, bathed in the city's special light, are some of the most renowned. The cupola in the foreground was not wrapped by artist Christo; the city government is restoring a historic monument that lost its top in a storm. Its red-domed twin is intact. High in the center, the cupola of the Palacio Barolo dominates the skies of downtown Buenos Aires.

ABOVE *In front of the Biela Café, one of the city's most popular meeting places, a red London-like phone booth stands as a colorful monument to the privatization of the Argentine government-owned telephone company, now in more efficient hands.*

OPPOSITE *The Torre de los Ingleses (Tower of the English), in the style of Big Ben, was a gift from Great Britain to Argentina in honor of its centennial. Ambrose Poynter, an English engineer, designed the tower in 1916.*

in the country's economic development. There is a rich bibliography in the English language dating back two hundred years that catalogs the incredible growth of the city and the changing views of those who came to see the "greatest city south of the equator," the "Paris" or "Athens of America," the "Babylon of the South," or the "white man's city of South America," as different writers have labeled it.

The text brings back the glory of the city's golden age, without the wrinkles and warts so apparent in the untouched photograph of today. The city has so many idiosyncrasies: more psychoanalysts than New York; record tobacco consumption (at the beginning of the century, for example, the Bank of the Argentine Nation spent $100,000 in one year on cigars for the institution's directors), with two tobacco companies ranking among the nation's top ten in terms of sales, along with oil companies, automobile manufacturers, and steel mills; more hotel beds for rent by the hour than in any other major city; world leader in meat and fourth or fifth in wine consumption; and any number of other unexpected record-breaking eccentricities.

Foreign chroniclers have often been overenthusiastic or overcritical in their judgments about the city and its inhabitants. Argentine observers can be accused of the same debility. While the photos give a singular vision of the city, the text gathers a multiplicity of opinions, offering an overview of what went on at the sites of many of the pictures during the country's heyday.

A city is more than the sum of the anecdotes that can pinpoint its idiosyncrasies; its soul cannot be captured on color film, no matter what the natives of more primitive societies believe. It takes effort and intuition to go soul-searching. It also takes perception and patience to maintain the necessary neutrality and avoid accepting what are passed off as tried-and-true clichés.

The photographs and text in this book reflect a fragment of the city—two observers' visions, each complementing the other to give the reader a more profound feel for Buenos Aires, a city that for its first century of existence seemed doomed to be a forgotten backwater at the far edge of Europe's collective imagination, and yet in its third century—turning the tables on the past—vied with New York as the Promised Land for millions of Europe's destitute. Today it is no longer a forgotten wilderness, nor is it the paradise it seemed back in 1910, when John Foster Fraser could title a book *The Amazing Argentine, a New Land of Enterprise.*

Edward Shaw
Madreselvas
Costa Brava, Chile
January 1998

proper portion of a steer to assuage their hunger. Beef has, of course, remained a priority in the porteño's diet, and while per capita annual consumption has fallen to two hundred pounds, one must keep in mind that the figure includes both infants and the toothless. The average Argentine consumed at least a pound a day until the fashion in nutrition decreed that too much meat was unhealthy. To compensate, Argentina became the world's fifth-largest wine producer but virtually refused to export any, determined first to satisfy domestic demand.

The first strokes of an impressionist portrait begin to appear: waves of immigration displacing or incorporating a rather small native population; a minute society of ambitious Spaniards cast away in a far-off corner of the globe, frustrated and forsaken, with no gold-bearing natives to fulfill their dreams, and nothing to do but catch cattle and wait for contraband to arrive. The passage of a pair of centuries produced an alluring breed of women who captivated the fancy of many a visiting adventurer, and the deprived local conditions fomented a certain tendency toward extravagance and swagger when possible.

By the time Charlotte Cameron came to visit the city at the beginning of this century, things had changed considerably, and she arrived with eight pieces of baggage—counting the steamer trucks but not her hatboxes—in an attempt to keep up with the natives.

In her book *A Woman's Winter in South America* (1910), she recommended that a traveler take "a wardrobe with well-cut coats and skirts of grey, blue, or any shade of alpaca or tussore silk. . . . Foulards are also most useful. Of course, white linen and lingerie frocks look very pretty and cool, but the laundry bills are rather high, as are labour and all things in this new El Dorado. The Argentine ladies are beautifully dressed. They spend large sums on their toilettes; no expense is spared. In Bond Street, the Rue de la Paix (Paris), or the Graben (Vienna) one will not see more elaborate costumes. And the ladies of B.A. are very handsome; their large, dark eyes and proud Spanish bearing makes them distinguished among the beauties of the world."

In her book, Cameron touched on three aspects that remain constants in any chronicle of life in Buenos Aires. First and foremost is the magnificence of the city's women; second is the care and effort taken to look one's best in any circumstances; and third is a marked tendency toward extravagance and ostentation. Porteños are enthusiastic and often compulsive consumers, to the delight first of English smugglers, then of Parisian couturiers and art dealers, and more recently of Miami malls and Manhattan department stores.

What with its humble beginnings and severe growing pains, who could imagine that Buenos Aires was to expand into the largest Latin city south of the equator (now outstripped by São Paulo) and the Athens (or Paris, take your pick) of the Americas? This is even more surprising when reading Father Sepp's description of the scant importance given to the local architecture at the end of the seventeenth century. "Houses and Churches here are not built of Brick, but Clay, not above one Storey high; and this not so much for want of Stone, but of Lime and Mortar; the burning of which has been but lately set up here, as well as the making of Tiles and Bricks some Years before. They have since that time begun to build a Steeple of Brick, which is near half finished, and intend soon to begin a new Church of the same material. The Jesuits themselves are the Architects, and the Work-men, certain *Indians* sent thither from the Cantons [Jesuit communities] in the Country.

When Charlotte Cameron visited Buenos Aires at the turn of the century, she was struck by how expensively and beautifully dressed the Argentine women were, as this gathering of women at the Hippodrome attests.

An 1819 watercolor by the artist Emeric Essex Vidal shows the architecture of Buenos Aires at that time.

The Castle itself, where the Governour resides, is only of clay, surrounded with an Earthen Wall; and a deep Trench." As Jorge Luis Borges, Buenos Aires's most universal author, wrote in a poem, "They set up a few tremulous ranches along the coast and fell asleep homesick."

The tradition of impermanent building continued well into the nineteenth century. The city boasts no spectacular colonial architecture, such as the marvels to be found from Mexico City to Santiago, and even in the central Argentine city of Cordoba. An authoritarian governor in an adobe "castle," a bevy of self-declared architect-priests bent on instant conversion, and a gluttonous native population provided the core for the identity of what was soon to become a city that rivaled New York a century ago as a probable paradise for Europe's distressed.

In the process of developing a taste of its own, the city became a spicy stew of contrasting and at times conflicting flavors. While the porteños yearned to define their national character and struggled to forge a unique identity, the rest of the world reduced Argentina to a series of clever clichés and sterile stereotypes. Tango; soccer; eccentric rulers (Perón and his tandem of wives, Evita and Isabelita); meat and wheat; polo; Latin-class lovers; boxers like Firpo and Bonavena; international idols like Jorge Luis Borges, Che Guevara, and soccer star Diego Maradona (a topic of conversation even in Myanmar), tennis champ Vilas, golf champ de Vicenzo, and five-time Formula One winner Fangio; chronic instability and postponed promise have been the themes of the occasional article in the press or, more recently, the rare report on cable TV.

What in fact differentiates a porteño from a New Yorker, a Parisian, or a resident of Rio or Mexico City? Argentines in general have gained fame far in excess of their numbers and have also been the subject of more comments by more foreign observers than the inhabitants of any other country in South America. The range of reactions is as broad as the River Plate.

Gabriel García Márquez is attributed with declaring, "The human ego is the little Argentine inside us all." The Argentine's arrogance when traveling within the hemisphere is similar to that ascribed to the German several decades ago. In Europe and the United States, his extravagance is the most frequent characteristic to be observed. "Give me two!" was for years the motto of the Argentine shopper in malls and department stores in the northern hemisphere.

At home, the porteño is a more complex individual. Visitors have cited a wide variety of facets of the difficult-to-define national character. Many are enlightening; others are far-fetched. In *Silver Seas and Golden Cities: A Joyous Journey through Latin Lands* (1931), the well-known writer Frances Parkinson Keyes called her experience in Argentina in 1931 a stimulating one: "I found its atmosphere delightful and its people cultured, charming, and wholly hospitable." For the segment of society that the traveler is apt to meet, her evaluation is still right on target today.

Turning to the female inhabitants of what was once the largest city in Latin America, Rosita Forbes informed her readers in *Eight Republics in Search of a Future* (1932) that "the Argentine woman is never

dull. She can put into words the things people in other nations leave unsaid." Moving on to the men, she evolved the following theory: "Argentine men present a curious mixture of qualities and defects. They are apt to combine the wit of France and the pride of Spain, with the intransigent temper of the Irish and the alertness of the North American. They have the diffidence, the optimism, and the sensitiveness of the very new, the sorrows and the inherited misconceptions of the very old." Doña Rosita's experience was perhaps limited to a reduced circuit of outspoken ladies and hesitant men.

Thomas Turner, a writer who lived in Buenos Aires from 1885 to 1890, summed up porteño men in *Argentina and the Argentines* (1892): "Male Argentines are, generally speaking, handsome-featured, under-sized, and effeminate. In manner and dress they affect French fashions, and do it indifferently well. The unmarried Argentine is a born dandy. He announces his presence by a hundred perfumes; and his symmetrical moustaches, twisted to invisible points; his immaculate linen, his jeweled fob, his rings and studs, his gold-headed malacca, his patent-leather boots or shoes tapered to an agonizing point, his flowered vest, and his gorgeous cravat, show that his chief care in life is the adornment of his exquisite person. He is clever, witty and showy—all sparkling facets, but eminently superficial. As a companion he is lively, affable, and unreliable. He is proud, but not haughty, intolerant of dullness and impatient of virtue. You will not easily find an Argentine who is fond of work or who does not mind soiling his fingers with anything but ink." This sketch of the men of the River Plate is no longer an accurate one, of course, but it serves as a revealing backdrop for discovering the character of the porteño of today.

An Anglo-Porteño's vision of Argentine womanhood in the 1880s is cited by Turner. "It is

*English author W. H. Koebel's obser-
vation that Argentines have "an
intense desire to cut a dashing figure
wherever they may find themselves" is
illustrated in Pellegrini's 1841 painted
lithograph of the Church of San
Francisco.*

said that when Venus was dispensing her gifts
among her sisters, she gave prominence in grace
and elegance to the Spanish women; to the Italian
perfection of form and feature; in liveliness and
savoir-faire to the French woman; to the English
woman a complexion as clear as the morning, and so
on—some special gift to the women of everywhere
on earth; but she forgot the *porteña* altogether, till
being reminded of her neglect, she took from each
woman of every race a fragment of the special
perfection of each one of them and bestowed it

upon the *porteña*, thus creating a race of women
unequalled in the variety of their charms in any
other country under the sun." Several generations
later, many of us agree with the unknown Anglo-
Porteño of a rampantly poetic nature.

Reverend Charles Currier contributes to our
survey his observations of Argentine women, made
in 1911 in his book *Lands of the Southern Cross:* "One
very useful occupation of the ladies of Argentina is
the management of public charities, which is, generally, in their hands. . . . The ladies are less mascu-

line than ours; but they would possess still more grace, were they to use less powder and paint, a disquieting custom that prevails generally."

The ladies of Buenos Aires are as active as ever in creating and running charitable organizations, and much to the good Reverend Currier's posthumous relief, paint and powder, though still major items in most porteñas' budgets, are applied with greater discretion today.

In *The Great South Land*, English author W. H. Koebel said of the Argentines in 1915, "They are a pleasant people to meet, whose interests usually fail to carry them far outside the frontiers of dress, an ambition to mix in the titled society of other lands, a keen appreciation of the merits of bridge and the points of a racehorse, and an intense desire to cut a dashing figure wherever they may find themselves. They have long been noted for kindliness and for a charm of manner that is very real; but at the same time they retain a certain amount of the *laisser-faire* of the South. Thus at a large dinner-party you may reasonably expect to find two or three places vacant of their expected guests, either because they have forgotten the engagement, or because they have forgotten to tell their host that they have remembered that they cannot come!"

To round out this fascinating, if unscientific, examination of the Argentine character, here is an excerpt from former United States ambassador James Bruce's book *Those Perplexing Argentines*. In a chapter titled "The Family Is Everything," Bruce describes a meal: "Sit down at dinner with a typical Argentine family, whether the family is poor, middle class, or in the landed *estanciero* group, and several things will probably strike you at once. Your host's mother will be in the place of honor. Children old enough to sit up by themselves will have chairs. The table itself will be dressed with the finest linens and silver the family can afford. No matter how poor the host he will probably serve several courses. And in nine cases out of ten you will have wine. Papa is head, mama is his deputy, and *his* mother, as the oldest and most respected member of the circle, is the queen. Under the 'father rule' set up by the civil code, papa has long exercised the same kind of unlimited and unquestioned authority so often employed by the President of the Republic in running the government."

If Buenos Aires is viewed from afar with a mixture of ignorance, curiosity, and astonishment, how do those who were born and reside there feel about their city? One vital ingredient is the love-hate syndrome of the passionate. Another is the melancholy of the misplaced—that aching to anchor the past in the present. A third is the pomposity of the insecure. Porteños deep down doubt that Buenos Aires is still all that the delighted visitor decrees it to be. To hide their doubts and misgivings, residents criticize the city as they would their spouses, with an underlying tone of affection. But beware, if a foreigner follows suit, he is immediately reminded that he is but a guest at their table and not entitled to voice his negative opinions.

In a word, living in Buenos Aires is what you make it. You start with a number of crucial pluses. The climate is temperate and can be invigorating most of the year. The seasons come and go much as they do in the Carolinas or southern France. The natives complain of the humidity; some foreign observers even blame their often gloomy mien on the high degree of dampness. Echoes of the glories of the tropics abound: palm trees and bougainvillea brighten the dismal stucco tone that characterizes the city. There are no dangerous insects, snakes, or animals, nor are there long spells of extreme heat or cold.

When of a mind to be so, the population is motivated and proficient, capable of all that their ancestors from the Old World did so competently. Once totally isolated from all that they yearned to imitate, porteños are now just an electronic pulse-beat from anywhere, and an overnight plane ride can get you anyplace except Asia. When things are looking bright, Buenos Aires *is* the best of all possible worlds, especially today, when urban decay, pollution, violence, and overcrowding threaten the viability of so many of the world's once user-friendly metropolises.

"Buenos Aires doesn't look like Europe; it looks like pictures of Europe—like a Spain or Italy a homesick immigrant might see in a dream," editor Kathleen Wheaton writes in the 1996 *Insight Guide* on Buenos Aires. The city is, in many ways, a template of make-believe. Everything is so evanescent, so unsettled, that anyone can reinvent the surroundings he wants. Given such fluid circumstances, it is surprising that the porteño did not develop his environment with more fantasy, with greater imagination. Writer Eduardo Crawley observed, "Buenos Aires play-acts at being a city that really belongs in the northern hemisphere, and, although it somehow drifted down to the South Atlantic, it is still attached to the parental body by an imaginary umbilical cord."

Rooms with a view penetrate the skyline above the deep blue waters of the lake in Palermo Park. A small boat called a biciscafo *permits a young couple to drift in solitude beneath the palms that dot the shore and protect visitors from the clamor of nearby city streets.*

CHAPTER 2

Kilometer Zero

Buenos Aires covers some 77 square miles (200 square kilometers). Almost square, it has a perimeter of 37 miles (60 kilometers), and lies at 34° 36′30″ south latitude and 58° 22′19″ west longitude. The population within the city limits is more than 3,000,000, with 300,000 more women than men. There were more inhabitants in 1947 than there are today. The population of the suburban semicircle that rims the city has grown to 8,000,000, making the consolidated urban complex the eighth largest in the world.

Built on the banks of the River Plate, the city was set out in a grid pattern, forming checkerboard blocks that measure 400 feet (120 meters) on each side. This model, imposed by urban planners back in Spain, did not consider the site's most obvious asset—its location along the shore of the world's widest river. Early settlers seemed to want to forget the hellish time spent crossing the Atlantic and built what is basically a landlocked town. Whereas Montevideo and the Brazilian cities facing the ocean integrated the coastline into the everyday life of the population, Buenos Aires gave no importance to its riverfront until recently. While many of the better suburbs run along the river to the north, the rows of high-rise

The Obelisk at the intersection of Corrientes and 9 de Julio avenues in the center of Buenos Aires, often mistakenly thought to be Kilometer Zero, was erected in 1936 to commemorate the four hundredth anniversary of the city's founding.

The Plaza of the Congress, where the marker of Kilometer Zero is located (obscured here by the trees), is one of the city's largest plazas. It is also unfortunately one of the least cared for. Neither federal nor municipal authorities respond to residents' or tourists' complaints about its decay.

apartments right on the water—so common in most waterfront cities—are nowhere to be seen.

As is the case in most large urban complexes, there has been a pronounced tendency to move from downtown to less densely populated suburban areas. Every porteño dreams of owning his home, and a high percentage of them manage to convert this priority into reality: more than 70 percent of the population lives in a family-owned home—whether a châteaulike mansion in the northern

suburb of San Isidro worth millions or a $25,000 one-room apartment in one of the dozens of middle-class neighborhoods that sprawl across the flat, uniform surface of the city.

When one takes into account that home mortgages did not exist until recently, becoming a property owner required tenacity and patience or a generous relative. In a land with a minuscule stock market and an erratic government bond market, most savings went into "bricks," as the porteño puts it. First one acquires a home in the capital, Buenos Aires's official role in the national administration; second, a vacation home on an Atlantic beach, either in Argentina or Uruguay; third, a small weekend home just beyond the border of the suburbs; fourth, an *estancia*, or ranch; and finally, an apartment in Miami, New York, or Paris. Once the housing infrastructure is taken care of, any surplus funds might find their way in part into the local stock market. What with time-sharing, resort packages, the soaring cost of taxes and maintenance, and growing insecurity, the trend, however, is shifting toward living in high-security apartment buildings and closed residential communities.

The centennial of Argentina's independence occurred in 1910, and it was a year for celebration. The city had consolidated its image as a metropolis to be reckoned with, and many of the buildings, parks, and avenues that catch the eye of visitors today date from that moment. It was an age of elegance and opulence. Homes were built to look like castles—and they still do. As in New York, most of these solid buildings are now the headquarters of official or institutional entities. The rich may have gotten richer, but they no longer use their fortunes to create monumental residences in the center city. Some build extravagant homes in the suburbs, while others opt for the anonymity and security of luxurious, spacious floors in apartment buildings.

Cities tend to be aimless creatures, sprawling irrationally in response to the whims of style and demands of developers. Buenos Aires is no exception. The city started in the south where the Plate joins the Riachuelo, a stream now contaminated by industrial waste, in the area called La Boca. It then marched north, the powerful leading the way. Commerce followed, and business, slower to react

to change, also gradually shifted its operations northward along the riverfront until it hit the railway lines and a series of green spaces that provide the average porteño, trapped in an endless maze of high rises and narrow, crisscrossing streets, the opportunity to remember that his city is really built at the edge of the world's widest river.

If we start at what Argentines consider to be the hub of their city—Kilometer Zero—the point from which mileage markers across the country spread out, we find ourselves at the northeast corner of the Plaza of the Congress. The plaza is named for the two different congressional conventions called to create the country, and all that occurs there serves as a characteristic cross section of life in downtown Buenos Aires.

Just a few yards away from the small obelisk that designates the exact point of Kilometer Zero, and unrecognized by the majority of those passing by, stands an original cast of Auguste Rodin's *The Thinker*. Near Rodin's bronze masterpiece is a site reserved for a statue of Juan Domingo Perón, but the project, like so many in Buenos Aires, remains unfunded. This juxtaposition reflects two constant characteristics of the society: incredible treasures from the past and unrealized projects awaiting better times in the future.

The highlight of the plaza, and of the city itself, is the building that houses the nation's Congress. Travel writer Henry Stephens, in his book *Journeys and Experiences in Argentina, Paraguay, and Chile,* declared in 1920 that the Congress building, erected in 1907, "is the finest building in South America. It cost $20,000,000, also making it the most expensive building on the continent. All the marble for its facing was imported from Italy."

Above the building's immense portal, just below the cupola, is an enormous sculptural group in bronze depicting a powerful lady—a mythological

borrowing representing Liberty—gamely trying to rein in a pair of furious stallions pulling her chariot helter-skelter in the direction of Argentina's White House, known here as the Casa Rosada because it is painted a peculiar shade of pink. Many differing political interpretations have been given to the beleaguered lady and her steeds. The Congress and the Casa Rosada stand facing each other, connected by the mile-long, tree-lined Avenida de Mayo.

On a corner adjacent to Congress is a bizarre ten-story building with a windmill at the top. El Molino, as the structure is called, is now in total disrepair, and the smart café that once thrived on the ground floor, catering to senators and tourists alike, was recently closed, its large plate-glass windows blindfolded. Two larger-than-life-sized statues of blackamoors who once hammered on an enormous bell to sound the hour, much to the distress of nearby neighbors, adorn a nearby building.

When the country has a democratically elected government, it is in the cafés surrounding Congress that Argentine politicians gather and decide the fate of the country. Knowing that the second, and more pervious, seat of power is here, anyone with

LEFT When officially inaugurated in 1908, the Congress building was the most expensive building ever undertaken in Latin America. In front of it is a major monument presided over by a female figure symbolizing the Republic; it was created by two Belgian artists in the 1910s.

BELOW Atop the portal of the Congress building a feisty amazon in the guise of Liberty struggles to rein in a pair of unruly Argentine horses.

ABOVE *The Molino (Windmill) Building is a national landmark that rivals its neighbor, the Congress, as a favorite in porteño folklore. The café at the corner has always been a popular gathering place for politicians and hangers-on.*

RIGHT AND BELOW *A turn-of-the-century French staircase connects reception rooms on the second floor with the Molino Café, a delightful spot for coffee and the wonderful pastries the proprietors specialized in creating. The landmark building is patiently awaiting a much-needed restoration.*

OPPOSITE *Cupolas are a constant delight for pedestrians who lift their line of vision; they do so at their own risk, however, as sidewalks are invariably perilous. The cupola in the foreground has since been repaired by the city government; its portholes and lightning rod are once again intact.*

RIGHT *"Enough is enough" reads the banner of a group of art students protesting the injustices of the day in front of the Casa Rosada. The most frequent protesters are pensioners and schoolteachers. Both groups have regularly scheduled weekly rallies to press their claims.*

a gripe brings it to the plaza. Unlike London, lone speakers are rare. Usually protests are made in groups, and as a rule each group repeats its demands on a certain day every week. Pensioners gather on Wednesdays, blocking traffic and presenting their point of view on loud, scratchy microphones.

Life around the plaza, often at fever pitch during the demonstrations, also has its domestic side. Down the street from the Molino Café, an imaginative porteño built himself a typical California-style house atop a tall apartment building. Beneath it and beside it, an Art Deco cinema has recently been split into three.

Nearby, a vast turn-of-the-century stucco building, recently abandoned by the Ministry of Labor, was bought from the state by a developer and is being recycled into a hundred apartments and offices. The marketing of the renovated building has become a landmark in local real estate history, because this is the first project in the downtown area designed to refurbish a historical building and offer it as apartments. The scheme was so successful that every unit was sold on the day the palatial building, with its fifteen-foot-high ceilings, was advertised in the two leading newspapers, *Clarín* and *La Nación*. The building, like so many in the neighborhood, has a spectacular cupola, which was sold for $200,000.

Adjacent to the building is one of Buenos Aires's oldest theaters, the *Liceo*. Managed by an American for a long time, it is still operating. In front of it, along the short spell of sidewalk between Rivadavia and Avenida de Mayo, an outdoor café, the Piazza, provides tourists and habitués with excellent coffee and honey-dipped croissants. On Sundays one can discover the political leanings of clients by the newspaper they are reading: the most conservative are engrossed in *La Prensa* or *La Nación*, the less adamant in their views wade through the thick tabloid *Clarín* and those leaning to the left study *Página 12*.

Above the café, at the corner of Avenida de Mayo and Luis Saenz Peña Street, a large 1950s apartment complex rises, crowned by a series of towers that presage Italian architect Aldo Rossi's ubiquitous postmodern solution to topping otherwise soulless blocks of steel, concrete, and glass. Across Avenida de Mayo from this building is one of the delights of Buenos Aires's architecture: La Inmobiliaria, a block-long apartment house in a mock-Italianate style, built in 1910. Fifty-foot red cupolas crown the east and west ends of the building, each owned by a New Yorker, one who came to tango and the other who settled in Buenos Aires in the 1960s.

The plaza in front, which covers three square blocks, is in a distressing state of abandonment. Recently the city bolstered the lighting, so that from the far end a pedestrian can now make out the silhouette of the Congress building three blocks away. The city's most important building itself is lighted only by whim—when the caretaker takes a fancy, when the favorite soccer team of someone in power wins a championship, or for several hours on the eve of a national holiday. When the lights are turned on, the spectacle is breathtaking.

LEFT *In the cupola of a building where Avenida de Mayo ends and the Plaza of the Congress begins, a well-traveled collector of primitive art has spread part of his collection around the room in search of a proper spot for each object.*

ABOVE *One of the fabulous cupolas of the Inmobiliaria Building, designed in 1910 by Italian architect Luigi Broggi, has been refurbished recently by a New Yorker, Pryor Dodge, who uses his spacious terrace to practice the tango, the passion that keeps luring him back to Buenos Aires.*

ABOVE AND RIGHT *Artist Miguel D'Arienzo's large studio is located in downtown Buenos Aires. A whimsical mural of country life wraps around one corner, while studies for paintings and works in progress fill another and serve as a perfect backdrop for the artist to pose with his German shepherd and some of his other models.*

While Avenida de Mayo itself has traditionally been home to many of the city's diehard Spanish community, the apartment buildings ringing the plaza house a veritable cross section of the city's population. Blessed with their spectacular view of presidential visits and periodic parades, they are disturbed only by the Wednesday marches, when protesting pensioners walk noisily across the plaza to press their claims in front of Congress, and during general strikes and other similar instances of civic strife. The long-suffering residents range from writers, journalists, artists, and theater people to old retirees, who moved there in more sober times.

A disconcerting variety of dogs circulate freely in the plaza, while their masters converse or sit reading on benches. Cats scurry along the side-

BELOW *The patio of this century-old house in Constitución, a downtown neighborhood near one of the major train stations, is one reason why the owner chose to move here from the city's more chic residential areas.*

LEFT *The living room is recovering from the visit of an unruly guest—the seat in the French chair is being reupholstered. Otherwise, the room exhibits its customary elegance.*

RIGHT *The dining room with its black-and-white checkerboard floor opens onto the lush patio. Rustic country furniture gives the room a relaxed, informal feeling that belies its downtown setting.*

Portholelike apertures, reminiscent of windows tucked into French mansards, light this cozy corner, with its fireplace and shelves of favorite books and treasured objects.

walks, and pigeons by the legion flock to the smaller fountains or fly in ragged formation overhead, roosting on rooftops or window ledges, to the annoyance of Galician janitors.

For the visitor, much of the charm of Buenos Aires life can be assimilated in a few hours of concentrated observation seated in a café on the perimeter of the Plaza of the Congress. An important portion of life in downtown Buenos

OPPOSITE *Architect and artist Jacques Bedel's architectural studio opens onto the covered courtyard of his turn-of-the-century home/atelier in Constitución. His large sculptures stand in sharp contrast to the scale of the maquette of a building on his worktable.*

BELOW *A corner of Bedel's atelier displays several of his spherical sculptures and a number of works from his series of "Books." Bedel put his talent as an architect to good use in redesigning the space and volume of his home.*

Aires occurs in the street: shopping, walking the dog, reading on a park bench, discussing the fine points of rough-and-tumble local politics over an "espresso-sized" rather bland cup of coffee, or just strolling and inspecting everyone else.

Time is still relatively elastic in Buenos Aires, and unpunctuality is part of the daily routine; even not showing up at all, after accepting an invitation, is tolerated. Porteños don't make a point of planning ahead. If you invite someone for dinner more than a few days in advance, you must confirm the day before, or even the same day, to be sure your invitation has not been superseded by a more recent or enticing one.

The Congress building, once known as the Palace of Gold because of its exorbitant cost, was erected to face Government House—also called the Palace of Gold by prior generations—a mile down Avenida de Mayo. The Avenida cut a wide swath through the center of the city, eliminating a dozen blocks of buildings to permit its construction. The once elegant avenue was inaugurated with a parade of five hundred torch-bearers on July 8, 1894, and opened to carriages to celebrate Independence Day the following day.

Now, sadly, the Avenida has fallen on hard times, but in 1913 Annie Peck informed her readers in her book *The South American Tour,* "It is considered by some the finest street in this hemisphere, others prefer the Avenida Rio Branco in Rio, while all those who admire skyscrapers will insist that it is not to be compared with New York."

And almost a century ago Delight S. Prentiss could crow, "In the Avenida de Mayo, the best street, the French style of buildings of uniform height, a row of trees, the cafés with their sidewalk tables, the handsome shops and those little islands of refuge that save your life when crossing the crowded streets, all strongly suggest the boulevards of Paris."

Fifteen years later, Harvard graduate Henry Stephens countered, "The Avenida de Mayo is physically somewhat similar to the Parisian boulevards, but in character it is widely different. If it is supposed to ape them, it is then a poor imitation, but so different is it in most respects, that as a first impression I would only call it a physical imitation. The oftener and the longer one sits in front of the cafés and watches the people pass by, the further apart he draws the comparison of the street to any street in the world. I would designate the Avenida de Mayo as original."

The city's oldest café is the Tortoni, founded more than a century ago. The café caters to an amusing mix of intellectuals, music lovers, and tourists. "It was in front of this café that my acquaintances came at least twice a day," Stephens wrote, "and from a marble-topped iron table beneath the street awning we observed Bonaerense (porteño) life to great advantage as it paraded by. We soon became so accustomed to the different passers-by, many of whom went by at the same time each day, that we soon knew the vocations of many of the folk that were but atoms in the large population of the great city." Those same marble-topped tables stand under a more recent version of the awning, and visitors still sit and sip espresso or draft beer. Today it is harder to determine the vocations of the passersby; all dress similarly and few carry the tools of their trade.

For more than thirty years, the Avenida, as it was known to all, was the center of life in the city; it boasted the most popular theaters, the most elegant hotels, the most stylish cafés. Vaslav Nijinsky, in the early days of his tortuous marriage; Le Corbusier, while discovering the city; and Federico García Lorca, when communing with local poets, all called the Avenida their home in Buenos Aires. On a good day at the Café Tortoni, for example,

ABOVE *A touch of Paris set against the deep blue sky of the Southern Hemisphere: intricate facades and ornate cupolas give Buenos Aires its European flavor in architecture.*

RIGHT *The Palacio Barolo is a mammoth honeycomb of a building on Avenida de Mayo. Italian architect Mario Palanti designed the bizarre facade and exuberant cupola in 1923.*

celebrity seekers could catch a glimpse of tango singer Carlos Gardel, Arthur Rubinstein, José Ortega y Gasset, or Josephine Baker.

"Meanwhile, its architecture, indifferent to human passions, accompanies the events from the majestic heights of the cupolas and pinnacles that adorn the Avenida with the eclectic splendor of all possible styles, as if wishing to symbolize a new cosmopolitan profile of the city. The aristocratic manner of the France of Louis XIV mixes with the bourgeois flair of Art Nouveau; the almost delirious anti-academic attitude of Palanti confronts the early geometry of Art Deco; the Central European perversion of the Viennese Secession complements the Italian neo-Renaissance revival of the Inmobiliaria Building. In this, its first great boulevard, Buenos Aires finally said, 'Anything goes!' There would be time later for pragmatism," writes the 1994 *Guía de Arquitectura* (Architectural Guide).

The most notorious example of "anything goes" is the Palacio Barolo, a wedding cake of an office building designed by Mario Palanti and finished in 1923. At the top, four hundred feet above the Avenida, a revolving searchlight emits a beam that can be seen in Montevideo, a hundred miles away. The anti-academic masterpiece was the tallest building in Buenos Aires for a decade.

The other unique building, located a block from the Plaza de Mayo, home of the Casa Rosada, is the former headquarters of Argentina's most distinguished newspaper, *La Prensa*. At the turn of the century the editor, José C. Paz, had the facade designed in Paris by the French architect Louis-Marie Henri Sortais. The construction of the monumental building was an international affair: French, Swiss, and American firms by the dozens contributed to enhancing the grandeur of the project. Paul Garnier created the enormous clock on the facade, above which rises a three-ton statue. Like the Statue

of Liberty, the figure holds a powerful torch in one hand, but in the other a sheet of newspaper. The building, along with many others along the Avenida, was recently restored by the city government, with financial assistance from Spain.

Plaza de Mayo dates from 1580, when Juan de Garay picked the site to be the settlement's Plaza Mayor, or principal plaza. Its present design, which is three blocks long and one block wide, dates from 1880, with renovations made in 1900, when French landscape architect Charles Thays gave the finishing touches to the classical symmetry imposed by his predecessor, Juan Antonio Buschiazzo. At its center, the Pyramid of May, commemorating inde-

José C. Paz built one of the world's most spectacular palaces for his newspaper, La Prensa. *Now the building houses the city's cultural bureaucracy. The Liberty-like figure crowning the structure is still one of the most photographed monuments in Buenos Aires.*

RIGHT *Called a* chorizo *(sausage)*
house, because all the apartments open
onto its long, narrow passageway,
this kind of building offers each resi-
dent a patio with its own piece of
pale blue sky. The bare bulb at the
entrance is still a fixture in many
porteño buildings.

BELOW *The Casa Rosada, seat of*
Argentina's executive branch, com-
mands a view of the Congress build-
ing twenty blocks up Avenida de
Mayo. The rear of the building
(shown here) overlooks the River
Plate.

pendence from Spain, is now dwarfed by the surrounding buildings, which include Government
House (Casa Rosada), the present version of which
was officially inaugurated in 1898; the Cathedral,
initiated in 1775, for which French sculptor Albert-
Ernest Carrier-Belleuse created the tomb of
General José de San Martín, the Liberator, and
Pedro Benoit the facade's neoclassical bas-reliefs,
inspired by the Palais Bourbon in Paris; the Banco
de la Nación, designed by Alejandro Bustillo in
1939 in the sober monumental style that characterized so many public buildings in the 1930s; and the
Cabildo (Town Council), dating from 1725. One of
the few extant colonial structures in Buenos Aires,
the Cabildo was reduced by a third when the Avenida de Mayo was built, and by another third when
a diagonal avenue was opened to the southwest, restoring its original symmetry in a reduced version.

Time and fashion shifted the heart of the city
northward along the river. By the 1930s the trend
was irreversible, and other avenues replaced the
Avenida de Mayo in prominence. The traditional
two-story houses and the tenement rental properties known as *conventillos*—series of one- or two-
room units, all opening on a common courtyard
—remained, but those who could moved into ten-
story apartment buildings to the north. The building code permitted structures to be as high as the
width of the street on which they were to stand.

Buenos Aires's golden age began to lose its
shine in the 1930s, and the Perón regime of the
1940s changed the social composition and comport-
ment of the Argentine forever. The small ruling
class lost its grip on the tiller, and the worker, both
blue and white collar, rallied behind Perón's prom-
ises to carve a bigger piece of the pie for followers.
The seemingly perfect blend of leisure and productivity, of Old World splendor and New World
dynamism, of beneficent wealth and dignified

The Cabildo, or Town Council, as it
looked in 1817, when Emeric Essex
Vidal painted this watercolor. One of
the few remaining colonial structures
in the city, it has been reduced to a
third its original size.

poverty, disappeared. The formula no longer functioned, and a new equilibrium had to be achieved. The adjustment is still in the works. Its aim is to accommodate each and every citizen in his or her new circumstances.

Certain events marked the inexorability of the transformation. The burning of the Jockey Club in 1953 was prophetic, a sign that nothing was sacred any longer. The subsequent burning of churches by radical Peronist groups proved the point. At a more prosaic level, the relocation of the Pedemonte Restaurant in 1980 signaled a return to more traditional values. Instead of being replaced by a fast-food franchise, the traditional businessmen's hangout for lunch moved all its wood-paneled walls to its new location nearby. The Jockey Club, however, moved north, and almost succeeded in re-creating its luxurious atmosphere in a pair of palatial mansions on the Plaza Pellegrini facing the fabulous French and Brazilian embassies. In spite of these noble efforts to hold back time, nothing will ever be quite the same again.

With that in mind, we can begin our journey out of the past and beyond yesterday's glories into the present: how porteños live, anchored to a great degree by the legacy of southern European Catholic and family-oriented values, but anxious to share in all the changes—cultural, social, and technological —that have swept across the globe in seismic waves.

Those whose families were part of the miraculous evolution of Buenos Aires into a pretender to the greatest-city crown a century ago still bask in often intact remnants of past brilliance. The halo of a Europe before it, too, lost its Old Worldness still casts its silhouettes over the city, especially the upscale residential and smart shopping areas we will visit on our journey—briefly south, then northward to the edge of the pampa—away from the original core.

OPPOSITE *The ornate facade of the Club Español, designed by Dutch architect E. Folkers in 1912, distinguishes it from the row of mundane office buildings along the Avenida 9 de Julio.*

CHAPTER 3

Public Buenos Aires

Moving to the southeasternmost point of Buenos Aires, we are in La Boca, where the first settlers landed. La Boca, meaning "mouth," is named for the point where a small stream, the Riachuelo, flows into the River Plate.

The district is a colorful corner, featuring houses built of rippled metal sheeting, originally appropriated from abandoned hulks of boats. The strident colors in which the houses are painted—green, violet, red, yellow, and blue—were also a result of the residents' abilities as scavengers. Unable to afford house paint, homeowners convinced local shipyards to give them leftovers of marine paint.

La Boca's early days in the last century were rough and ready, as Charles Domville-Fife, ex-correspondent of the *London Times* reported in his book *The Real South America* (1922): "The nightly murders of the eighties have given place to more subtle forms of crime. There was a time, however, when trained bloodhounds pulled venturesome riders from their horses in the Boca district, and when signs offering professional services were displayed by accomplished and highly respected assassins."

In 1882 a group of Genovese immigrants constituted the Independent Republic of La Boca and duly informed their king back

Rowboating through the lagoons of Palermo Park on sunny weekend afternoons is but one of the many pastimes the vast park offers city residents. This stretch of nature enhanced by French landscape architects and imported trees is located just blocks from downtown.

The colorful bridge control tower in La Boca, built in 1914, no longer functions; today it serves as just another structure on which to hang advertising, in this case, a banner offering courses in graphic arts.

Three bridges connect La Boca with the adjacent Province of Buenos Aires. The newest is part of a toll road to La Plata; the middle one, made of concrete in 1940, was once the biggest bridge in South America; the one in the foreground is no longer used.

in Italy of his new territory in the antipodes. General Julio Argentino Roca, hero of the Western Campaigns against the Indians and at the time president of the Argentine republic, rode into La Boca and, in a symbolic display of his power, removed the Genovese flag, thus reclaiming La Boca for Argentina. The next day the irrepressible Genovese named a street in his honor. The Independent Republic became an allegorical institution, devoted to community affairs and charity.

La Boca was the first stop for more than a million Italian immigrants, the majority of whom came from the area around Genoa. Many never left, so the predominant ethnic flavor is Italian. Several years ago a large Argentine corporation with roots in Italy spearheaded a program to rehabilitate parts of the neighborhood. Unfortunately, the Italian government did not support the initiative, leaving most of La Boca subject to ongoing decay.

One street, Necochea, catering to tourists both Argentine and foreign, is lined with gaudy cantinas that offer Neapolitan menus and boisterous sing-along entertainment. The stretch along the waterfront is in the process of being renovated: Techint, the Argentine-Italian concern dedicated to infrastructure projects all over the world, has organized an innovative cultural center, the Proa Foundation, and the city is about to revamp the local Museum of Fine Arts, the creation of a local painter, Benito Quinquela Martín.

La Boca floods periodically, so houses and sidewalks are elevated, the streets turning into miniature Riachuelos. A new cement barrier has been built along part of the waterfront to deter the advance of the unwanted waters. Gradually, the area is losing its decadent charm, though life is improving for the residents. Several artists have installed studios near the river, especially sculptors, who are delighted to have the space to spread out in.

TOP *A street lined with Neapolitan-style cantinas offers tourists seafood and pasta, rough red wine, raucous singing, and stale jokes. Sidewalks are raised high above street level, as La Boca tends to flood when strong winds attack from the southeast.*

CENTER *The brightly patterned exterior of the 3 Amigos fits into the spirit of this cantina, which offers customers nightly renditions of the tango.*

BOTTOM *As one moves beyond the bend in the Riachuelo, the authenticity of La Boca deteriorates into a row of brashly painted nightspots where the quality of the food and wine is relative and noise is the common denominator. But the area is now being renovated.*

ABOVE *Large slabs of stone await transformation into sculptures in Pablo Larreta's spacious workshop in La Boca. This waterfront district is home to many artists and the cutting-edge Proa Foundation, where excellent international art shows are held.*

RIGHT *Flanked by two of his sweeping stone carvings, Larreta stands amid a pile of beams salvaged from a recently demolished building.*

Although basically home to European immigrants, to the first steps of the tango, and to Argentina's most colorful soccer team, La Boca is also the place where one American made her mark. Caroline Maud, the daughter of Virginia slaves, a friend of Josephine Baker in New Orleans, and rootless, found herself opening a bar on Pedro de Mendoza Street near the corner of Almirante Brown Avenue at the turn of the century.

The bar, the Droning Maud, was a hangout for the likes of Jack London, Eugene O'Neill, and John Mansfield before they took to the pen. Caroline's only helper was Eve Leneve, mistress of the infamous Dr. Crippen, who murdered his wife,

was caught when attempting to escape with Eve, and was finally executed. Eve chose Buenos Aires to start a new life and found it among the diverse clientele at the Droning Maud.

La Boca is where the tango began. The heavy, haunting musical form—which can be played, sung, and/or danced—developed in the mid-nineteenth century at the fringes of the city as a response to new residents' search for a musical expression with which they could identify.

The component parts were *candombe*, brought by slaves from the western coast of Africa; flamenco from Spain; an Afro-Cuban rhythm introduced by sailors from the Caribbean; and the music that had gradually developed in the interior of Argentina. The common chord was nostalgia, a shared longing for a distant homeland.

The tango first started as a dance practiced by the men who gathered at cafés and brothels near the port. Little by little, lyrics, often bawdy, were added spontaneously, and the music began to find its own idiosyncratic form, complete with composers, orchestras, shows in theaters, and international acclaim.

Today, thanks to the tango's resounding success in France and Finland, Colombia and Japan, the music can be heard once again in Buenos Aires. The tango has been reincarnated in all of its multiple manifestations. It is danced on street corners for tourists; there are beautifully staged shows at elegant restaurant-cafés; enthusiastic combos and scratchy singers belt the sound out at corner bars; neighborhood clubs offer tango nights once a week

FAR LEFT *A neo-primitive mural in bas relief depicts a typical street scene in La Boca. A guitarist and a bandoneon player set the rhythm for a 1920s couple dancing a tango in front of the barrio's colorfully painted houses.*

TOP, CENTER, AND BOTTOM *On weekends, crowds gather to watch tango dancers go through their paces. Sportily dressed in black, this handsome couple bends and stretches with that perfect timing and harmony that gives the tango its sensual flavor.*

RIGHT *A trio of musicians—singer, bandoneon player, and guitarist—prepare to launch into a tango. The scene is a traditional one in La Boca, where the tango got its start at the beginning of the century.*

BELOW *Two period images of legendary tango singer Carlos Gardel beckon to new generations of fans. The top one is a rather kitsch rendition, but the bottom one could be considered the official portrait of the Zorzal (thrush), as he is affectionately known.*

where couples and singles gather with the sole intention of gliding around the floor, practicing the intricate steps of the mythical music.

The tango is played by a small group of musicians; the key instrument is a wailing bandoneon, or concertina, which sets the pace for guitars, flutes, violins, and if available, a piano.

The Frank Sinatra of tango, Carlos Gardel, is perhaps the city's most beloved citizen. Born in France or perhaps Uruguay, the Thrush, as his fans called him, died in a plane crash in Medellin, Colombia, in 1935. The porteño's favorite term for someone who is special is *Gardel.* You can still hear his recorded voice echoing through the streets in La Boca, a reminder that melancholy and nostalgia are still active components of the Argentine national character.

Tango is now one of the main tourist attractions. Charter groups of Europeans and Americans descend on the city for a week (or maybe forever), spend the days in strenuous classes with world-renowned teachers and the nights at the different clubs, each of which boasts a specific atmosphere and style.

One Boca tradition dwarfs all others: the local soccer team, Boca Juniors. Like the old Brooklyn Dodgers, the team, with its blue-and-gold uniforms and its singular stadium, is legendary. The team won its first national championship in 1919 and recently hired the mythical Diego Maradona to boost revenues. Boca fans are the most vociferous in the city, and the club's equally outspoken officials often get as much press as the players. Back in the early years, the commission could not agree on the team's colors. After interminable arguments, it was decided that the colors would be those of the flag of the next freighter to enter the port. The ship was Scandinavian, back when

Sweden and Norway were under a single flag, and the flag's colors were blue and gold.

The stadium, known affectionately as La Bombonera ("the candy box") because of its steeply stepped, opera house–style decks of seats, rises above the sheet-metal rooftops like the dome of a cathedral. One would expect the stadium—built between 1940 and 1944 on a plot thought to be too small for the purpose—to be the product of the imagination of an ingenious Italian, but in fact it was the initiative of Argentina's only well-known Slovene architect, Victor Sulcic.

San Telmo is another barrio, or neighborhood, that proclaimed its spiritual independence. The Independent Republic of San Telmo has attracted a few brave would-be bohemians from more middle-class areas of the city. Most are arts-related renegades, anxious to have more space and less overhead.

The barrio has never coagulated into a Tribeca, much less a Greenwich Village, although its Sunday antiques fair at the Plaza Dorrego does attract a cross section of porteño society and just about every visitor in town. Unfortunately, overpricing keeps the market from developing into a thriving affair like those in London or Paris.

In 1989 the city's Museum of Modern Art launched its new headquarters in an old tobacco

A future soccer star boots the ball high in the air as his younger brother looks on admiringly. Any free patch of green or stretch of pavement—even the tourist-filled streets of La Boca— is a potential soccer field.

ABOVE *The bookcase in musician Manolo Juarez's San Telmo apartment provides clues to his passions: framed Brazilian butterflies, one lone photo, four classical busts, stacks of video tapes, and a wide assortment of books.*

RIGHT AND FAR RIGHT *Another San Telmo resident, Martiniano Arce, the master of the city's* fileteros *(traditional Sicilian-style paintings using filigreed designs), now uses his craft to paint portraits of Argentine cult heros, such as Carlos Gardel and Evita Perón. A guitar, a vintage fan, and an old typewriter have also succumbed to the magic of his brush strokes.*

RIGHT *Artist/illustrator Hermenegildo "Menchi" Sabat is best known for his daily political caricatures in* Clarín, *Argentina's best-selling newspaper. He poses in his San Telmo studio in front of family photos, reproductions of his favorite paintings, and the tools of his trade.*

BELOW *Sabat's storage cubbyholes have the appeal of a Joseph Cornell box; a thank-you card, a box of glue, rollers, varnishes, photos, and a ball of string stand out in this geometrically designed display.*

RIGHT *A watercolor of a saxophone player testifies to Sabat's passion for jazz, while other works strewn about his studio reflect his incisive vision of Argentine politics.*

ABOVE *A Swiss family tree and a 1930s beauty in mock-Oriental glory are prime examples of the kitsch that abounds at the San Telmo fair.*

LEFT *A weapons vendor sits proudly before his display of knives, cleavers, and daggers, most of which have handles made from horn or antlers. Many of the utensils belonged to gauchos who used them to eat and frequently to fight.*

RIGHT *Dressed to match her merchandise, a vendor at the Sunday flea market in San Telmo shows how her artificial flowers can be put to good use adorning hats and slippers.*

LEFT *Old-fashioned glass soda bottles with their silvery siphons are popular collectibles that usually go for about ten dollars each.*

RIGHT *Old wooden stirrups covered in metal are authentic souvenirs of the country's turbulent rural past.*

BELOW *After a day at the San Telmo fair, the Plaza Dorrego Bar is a delightful spot to relax and chat over a drink and a handful of peanuts*

RIGHT AND BELOW *For generations, the Pallarols family has been designing and producing silver objects, ranging from plaques of chubby angels to bowls and plates. A sense of timelessness pervades their San Telmo workshop and is reflected in the masterly craftsmanship of the diverse objects they create.*

ABOVE *Imitating the northern European tradition of hanging a metal sign that depicts an establishment's wares, La Scala de San Telmo, a small theater-cum-café, sports a sign with a theatrical scene to alert passersby to its active program of concerts and performances.*

warehouse, and dozens of antique-cum-curio shops now line Defensa Street, spreading out from the Plaza Dorrego, which has become the barrio's epicenter, thanks to the resourcefulness and obstinacy of José María Peña, an architect who concocted the fair from scratch in 1970. For a dealer to get a permit for a stall, Peña has devised a periodic lottery in his stronghold, the funky City Museum, of which he is the first and perennial director. Thanks to his efforts, the area was declared a historic zone in the early 1970s.

As its upper middle class grew, Buenos Aires had to build an adequate infrastructure. The challenge was met with vigor and imagination. Many projects were designed to satisfy the recreational needs of this ever-expanding group. There were those projects with access to just the few, like the Jockey Club, others where the elite, to all effects, fenced itself off from the masses, such as the Colón Theater and the Hipódromo Argentino, the exclusive racetrack in the Palermo neighborhood. And there were others where all could mix, should they have

the desire, such as the Café Tortoni in the heyday of the Avenida de Mayo, the Biela and the Café de la Paix in the Recoleta today, and the spacious parks of Palermo. An outing to the nearby zoo or botanical gardens was, of course, an option available to all.

The original Jockey Clubhouse was as fine a town club as ever devised anywhere. "In many respects the Jockey Club stands alone amongst its kind throughout the world," wrote Koebel of the club in its prime. "There is a danger of verging on the wearisome in speaking continually of 'the finest in the world.' Yet, even without alluding to its exceptional features, the more ordinary attributes of the place lay claim to this title. The quiet magnificence of the building is less to be wondered at when the income of the institution from its racecourse and the percentage on the *pari-mutuel* is taken into account." In his book *Argentina* (1910), W. A. Hirst reaffirms the consensus. "The Jockey Club is probably unsurpassed by any Club building in the world." Rosita Forbes goes one step further. "The staircase of the Jockey Club is the eighth wonder of modernity," she states. Located on Florida near Lavalle, this architectural landmark, built in the 1880s, was burned as an act of supreme class retribution in 1953.

Another turn-of-the-century tribute to modernity was the extravagant use of electric lighting. A lamppost in front of Congress bears a plaque commemorating Thomas A. Edison and his incredible invention. The Jockey Clubhouse was "covered with an infinity of electric bulbs and no occasion to light these is ever allowed to pass unregarded. Often I have seen the building aglow like Aladdin's Palace in a Drury pantomime and scarce a soul in sight to feast his eyes on the outward magnificence of this great national institution which exists for the maintenance of the best breeds of man's devoted servant, the horse." This colorful vignette was English author J. A. Hammerton's take on the club's facade and raison d'être in his revealing book *The Real Argentine* (1915).

"This Club, noted as probably the richest in the world, has a famous Diana sculptured by Falguière on the first landing," Annie Peck informed her readers in 1913. "Corinthian columns, ornamentation of onyx, ivory and lapis lazuli are part of the decoration. A fine banquet hall, various dining rooms, luxurious drawing and reading rooms, rooms for cards, billiards, fencing, baths, etc., and a few to which ladies are admitted with a member for after-

The library at the exclusive Jockey Club on Plazoleta Carlos Pellegrini is one of the most sacrosanct spots in the city. Burned by rioters in the 1950s, the original Jockey Club on Calle Florida was abandoned for a safer site in Barrio Norte.

noon tea, unite to make this the equal of any Club-house in the world. Beautiful paintings and other expensive luxuries, like tapestries and carvings, attribute to the elegance of the establishment."

The Jockey Club symbolizes the porteño's commitment to English-style fraternizing, to thoroughbred racing stock, and to culture as a visual framework for displaying a society's durability. Everyone belongs to his favorite soccer club; only the elite, however, participate in the courtly rites of the Jockey Club.

Today's Jockey Club continues in a similar vein. In the December 1994 *National Geographic* John J. Putman describes the new clubhouse, which occupies two stately old mansions on Avenida Alvear: "There are rooms for snooker, bridge, poker, fencing, looking up one's geneaology, wagering on (and watching via television) races at the hippodrome, and many other activities. In this anachro-

nistic ambience, with cigar smoke and the click of chips and the slap of a masseur's hands, it seems the golden age persists." The only difference, and an anecdotal one at that, is the interest in fortifying the family tree; members back in the beginning were too busy planting trees to investigate ancestry.

The Colón Theater is also billed as one of the wonders of the New World, surpassing, in the minds of many, the Metropolitan in New York and the Opéra in Paris, and running neck and neck with Milan's La Scala for the title of the world's supreme opera house. The Colón has managed to maintain its international fame better than any other Argentine institution. Financed by the city and a foundation backed by wealthy music lovers, the majestic theater still attracts the best voices of all, and the most fashionable public at gala performances.

The inaugural gala performance took place on May 25, 1908, much later than had been expected when construction began in 1889. The project's first architect, Francisco Tamburini, who had just revamped the Casa Rosada, died on the job. His replacement, Victor Meano, who designed the Congress building, was assassinated in 1904 under circumstances no one was willing to discuss. One member of Congress moved for the demolition of the almost finished building, wanting to return to the original design. Finally, Jules Dormal, who had put the finishing touches on Meano's Congress, did the same for the Colón. The building ended up being designed by three architects in three styles, uniting Italian Renaissance with the solidity of German architecture and the grace and flair of French.

The Colón opened with Verdi's *Aida.* "That night those present, all of whom arrived elegantly attired, were delighted at the magnificence of the

Floor-to-ceiling bookcases of sumptuously bound books surround the reader who seeks knowledge or solace in the reading room at the Jockey Club. Few clubs in the world offer the facilities that are available to the members of Buenos Aires's most prestigious family club.

theater," Otilia Vázquez de Castro observed in her book *Las luces de Buenos Aires y sus tiempos* (1983).

In its uninterrupted career as host to the best, the theater has offered Caruso, Toscanini, Menuhin, and Callas, and continues to feature every artist of note. Five years after the grand opening Annie Peck wrote, "It has been said that the Argentines discover great singers; later they come to New York. The seats are more expensive than at the Metropolitan and the audience is as brilliant as any in the world." The latter two observations still hold true.

When it was off-season at the Colón, many of the season ticket holders climbed into their carriages or motor cars and were driven to the park at Palermo. The ritual lasted for several decades, until the rhythm of city life and the speed of the vehicles accelerated so greatly that the destination began to seem provincial in spirit. But in 1910, when the vogue was at its peak, Koebel wrote: "During summer the very pleasant custom exists of driving out to Palermo Park of an evening after the dinner function. Once within the park itself the spectacle is a fascinating one on such an

ABOVE *Red carpets welcome concertgoers to the foyer of the Colón Theater. In addition to an opera house and concert hall, the complex includes a museum, smaller spaces for more intimate performances, workshops, and fine artwork.*

FAR LEFT *The foyer at the Colón Theater fills with operagoers dressed in their best for a gala performance.*

LEFT *Inaugurated with a performance of Verdi's* Aida *in 1908, the Colón is one of the four most important opera houses in the world, along with the Metropolitan in New York, the Opéra in Paris, and La Scala in Milan.*

occasion. The avenues amidst the palms, eucalyptus, and poplar trees are thronged with vehicles to such an extent that, although the rows of these are frequently more than half a dozen deep, a walking pace is inevitable. The thousands of carriage lights moving slowly between the broader illuminations of the shaded avenues themselves lend to the scene an appearance of gaiety difficult to be surpassed."

The vast green space in Palermo, officially labeled the 3rd of February Park, was turned into a public park by President Domingo Sarmiento on the 1,235 acres of land that once belonged to his archenemy, Juan Manuel de Rosas, who had bought the property in 1839.

The park was modeled on the Bois de Boulogne in Paris and Hyde Park in London. Begun in 1874, it was finished by the French architect Jules Dormal in 1876 and enlarged between 1892 and 1913 by another Frenchman, Charles Thays, who was

ABOVE *The boxes at the Colón Theater maintain their Old World elegance, just as the performances at the opera house maintain their high standard of quality. These stalls are the preserves of season-ticket holders who come back year after year to the same seats.*

LEFT *The lights dim, the orchestra tunes up, the last operagoers rush to their seats just as the Colón Theater's gigantic curtain opens. There is rarely an empty seat at the Colón, especially for a gala performance like tonight's.*

responsible for much of the public landscaping in Buenos Aires.

When Rosas owned the property, a foreign visitor dubbed it the "Versailles of the pampa." Rosas was overthrown by General Justo José de Urquiza in the nearby town of Caseros on February 3, 1852, in the largest battle ever fought in South America, and the victor confiscated the property. His troops destroyed the gardens that Rosas and his wife had meticulously created, and Urquiza, on his sudden departure from the city following the battle of September 11, left Rosas's palatial mansion in ruins. Sarmiento demolished what was left of the Caserón, as the residence was known, and christened the park in honor of the day of Rosas's defeat.

By the end of the last century Palermo Park was another of the strongholds of porteño society. Let's take a look at the rise and fall of the park as a social phenomenon from 1900 to the 1920s.

In 1905 English travel writer Percy Martin observed: "Immediately after business hours everyone flocks to the beautiful Park of Palermo, and on any afternoon, but especially on Sundays and Feast Days, of which there are more than thirty in the course of the year, the place is invaded with carriages filled with showily dressed women and dandified men, the throng, slowly moving on account of its density, reminding one of Hyde Park on a day when Royalty is expected to pass by, or the Champs Elysées in the height of the season."

Jules Huret, a French observer, tells us in his *La Argentina,* first published in 1905, "Palermo is the one place for public get-togethers of the elegant society. . . . After five P.M., when the sun loses its strength, luxurious automobiles, superb carriages, and rental coaches race at full speed down Avenida Alvear to Avenida Sarmiento. But this lavish stream is not headed for the Park itself. The ceremony

has nothing to do with an outing in the fresh air, nor to deliver oneself to the solitary, comforting landscape. On the contrary, everyone is headed for Avenida Sarmiento, an avenue that is barely 400 meters long and planted in rather musty palm trees. In their wake, the fumes of petrol and of horse manure fill the air. . . . Everyone knows each other and greets one another ceremoniously. The foreigner is surprised by the silence of the multitude, by the affected seriousness, the grave immobility of the faces in contrast to the extraordinary vivacity of the eyes. Everyone stares intensely, with unexpected abandon. Evidently the men go to stare at the women, and the women to stare at each other. The other avenues remain deserted, and, how beautiful it would be to take a ride under the delicate green of the weeping willows, or the ombús, the eucalyptus and elms!"

A few years later an entranced Lord Bryce recorded his impressions in *South American Observations* (1912): "On fine afternoons, there is a wonderful turnout of carriages drawn by handsome horses, and still more of costly motor cars, in the principal avenues of the Park; they press so thick that vehicles are often jammed together for fifteen or twenty minutes, unable to move on. The ladies are decked out with all the Parisian finery and jewels that money can buy; and although nature has given to many of them good features and to most of them fine eyes, custom seems to prescribe that nature shall not be left to herself. Nowhere in the world does one get a stronger impression of exuberant wealth and extravagance."

Bryce continues, "The Park itself, called Palermo, lies on the edge of the city towards the river, and is approached by a well-designed and well-planted avenue. It suffers from the absolute flatness of the ground in which there is no point high enough to give a good view over the estuary,

Recalling Paris's Bois de Boulogne, with lakes, bridges, paths, and elaborately designed rose patches, the Rosedal garden in Palermo Park is a favorite escape from urban madness for porteños and visitors alike.

and also from the newness of the trees, for all this region was till lately a bare pampa. But what with its great extent and the money and skill that are being expended on it, the park will in thirty years be a glory to the city."

Charlotte Cameron was no less enthusiastic: "Palermo is the great playground for the Argentines, beautifully laid out with lakes, islands, and gardens. A great many blue gums flourish, and tropical trees of every kind abound. Here, late in the afternoon, when the *monde riche* promenade *en voiture,* you will find the ladies better dressed than in Hyde Park. The longest and most gorgeous feathers toss their plumage from well-turned-out automobiles, as if cost were a bagatelle. Rumors say they think nothing of paying twenty or thirty pounds for a hat."

By the 1920s Domville-Fife was able to offer a less elitist view of a day in the life of the park: "In this enclosure of 800 acres, there are one million trees, affording plenty of shade for the large lounging population, who are thus able to recline and smoke without becoming unduly hot or having their cigarettes extinguished by the rays of the sun."

In 1920 American writer F. A. Sherwood added a reference to the arrival of a more diverse

LEFT *Three elaborate stucco faces observe a frisky young elephant as he stretches in front of his century-old home at the zoo in Palermo Park.*

BELOW Cubanitos, *a crisp pancake filled with* dulce de leche, *Argentina's favorite dessert (made by boiling milk with sugar), are a popular snack enjoyed by young and old.*

BELOW *Bicycle-driven traveling markets offering children their favorite cookies, crackers, and soft drinks are a common sight in urban parks.*

public in his book *Glimpses of South America:* "The picture seems unreal, it is so perfect. . . . The electric lights are on now, and reflect in a riot of color on the waters of the lagoon. In their brilliancy, you amble on by one winding drive after another, and are more fully aware of the greetings that are exchanged between carriages, of laughing girls and the more formal elders, of the pleasure of seeing and being seen by one's friends, of the handsome turnouts, of the incongruous notes that are introduced into the spectacle of worn-out cars loaded to the gunwale with what are apparently not even middle classes, of Rolls-Royces and Fords, of the very latest French styles and of the most ragged of rags, of all the things that make up Palermo, at twilight."

Today Palermo is a playground for health enthusiasts: aerobics classes, t'ai chi groups, joggers, and walkers who waggle along like mechanical toys. A more sedentary segment of the city's population sit and sip the tealike drink maté, or just stretch out and sleep in the sun or in the shade, depending on the season. Traditional activities, such as soccer, picnicking, hugging, and pedal boating on the lake, animate the park on weekends. Palermo is the backyard of many a porteño. From the days of the original Signore Giovanni Domenico-Palermo, who had the good sense to marry an heiress and invest her inheritance in 1,235 acres of then open plain—including most of the park that bears his name—to today, the city's largest recreational space has reflected both the political and the social changes in Buenos Aires's balance of power.

The racetrack at the edge of Palermo Park is also a revealing barometer of the social changes in the city over the decades. The Hipódromo Argentino, inaugurated in 1876, was built in the best Belle Epoque style, similar in essence to Ascot and

The grandstand at the Hipódromo Argentino, built in 1876 in the elegant Belle Epoque style, maintains its original magnificence in spite of a decline in bettors' enthusiasm.

Longchamp. The tattersall—the building where auctions of racehorses are held—was designed by Italian architect V. Cestari and the members' pavilion by French architect Louis Fauré Dujarric. More than a century later, the sand track is still in excellent condition and the buildings retain their period beauty. Argentina continues to produce world-class thoroughbreds, many of which find their way to tracks and breeding farms in the United States. Artist Frank Stella, for example, has raised and raced Argentine horses with admirable success.

"Nothing in the United States approaches it," Annie Peck claimed in 1913. "While some Americans asserted that this was the finest Racing Ground in the world, a gentleman of Buenos Aires stated that it hardly equalled Longchamp. However, the *buildings* are superior."

One of the highlights of the seasons at the Palermo track is the periodic auctioning of yearlings, mares, and sometimes stallions. The occasional foreign buyer is often outbid by local trainers, usually buying on commission for one of the large stables or breeding farms. Racing's appeal has been diminished somewhat by off-track betting and television, but there are still enough racing fans to keep the track functioning and to create a traffic problem at every meet.

"Perhaps the favorite amusement of the capital is racing, for it appeals both to the love of horses and the love of gambling, which are two of the strongest predilections of the Argentines," W. A. Hirst pointed out in 1910. "The actual racing, though marred by inferior jockeyship, is extremely good, for the horses are of high quality and the runners are plentiful. The rich men of Argentina take great delight in bloodstock and many of the racers are by high-class English sires. This pursuit is often a source to them of pleasure as well as of profit."

A more recent vision of racing's impact on Argentine society is social historian Ezequiel Martínez Estrada's evaluation in his *X-Ray of the Pampa* (1933). "The hippodrome has three fundamental components: the aristocracy, which celebrates the genealogy of the thoroughbred, the nationals from the countryside with their totemic love for the horse, and the masses with their anxiety to tempt destiny with the wager."

The races now alternate between the old track in Palermo and a new, larger Jockey Club facility in the suburb of San Isidro. The breeding, training, and racing of thoroughbreds is still a passion of many, and not just of the wealthy as it was at the beginning of the century. One finds thoroughbred owners from every walk of life, attracted to the tradition by the strange thrill that racing your own colors ignites in many a man, and every now and again in a woman.

If most of the other "bests in the world" can no longer be claimed by Argentina, there is no doubt that Argentines are the world's best polo players. With a team sporting three Anglo-Argentine names and a lone Spanish one (Kenny, Nelson, Miles, and Padilla), Argentina won the first Olympic polo title when the sport was introduced at the games in 1924. Local teams have kept on winning ever since.

"If you attend a polo match in Buenos Aires, you will rub elbows with relatives and friends of the players themselves," writes Eric Weil in the 1996 *Insight Guide* for Buenos Aires. "They are the landed-gentry for the most part, 'beautiful people' who divide their time between the family *estancia* and elegant apartments in the city. Their dress code is casual elegance—sports coats, designer jeans, crisp shirts—and they watch the matches with the reserved demeanor of a crowd at a garden show. It is a world of belonging, one most Argentines have heard about but few have actually experienced."

International championships are held every November at the Campo Argentino de Polo in Palermo, across the broad expanse of Avenida del Libertador. Here, the top native players, along with the occasional player from overseas, vie to be recognized as the best team anywhere for that season. (Ten is the highest handicap a player can have. At present there are eight tens in Argentina.) Argentine polo ponies—now full-sized horses trained to bear the rough and tumble pace demanded by the game—are among Argentina's most celebrated exports, as are the younger players, who turn professional abroad and join teams everywhere from Brunei to Stony Brook, when the season arrives in those parts of the world.

The last site to be included in this brief overview of Buenos Aires's landmarks is the most spectacular of all. Cemeteries rarely make anyone's top ten,

ABOVE *The Campo Argentino de Polo (Argentine Polo Grounds) during a spring championship match. Residents of the nearby high rises have a birds-eye view of the game.*

LEFT *A hard-riding polo player, mallet high in the air, bears down on his fast-moving rival in an attempt to get control of the hard wooden ball.*

RIGHT *Adolfo Cambiaso is one of the outstanding young Argentine polo players who participate both as professionals and as amateurs on the tour, which takes them to the United States, Europe, and the Orient.*

ABOVE *A pair of polo players take a break from practice, leaving helmets, boots, spurs, and mallets on a swing at an estancia in the Pilar district of Buenos Aires Province, where several of the country's best teams have their headquarters.*

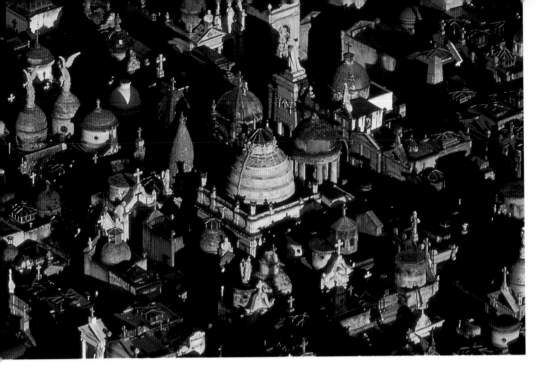

ABOVE *The chaotic skyline of the Recoleta Cemetery, one of Buenos Aires's most unique landmarks.*

OPPOSITE *From this bird's-eye view the Recoleta Cemetery looks like the grid pattern of a well-planned city. Any sense of uniformity quickly vanishes, however, when one walks along the broad streets and narrow alleys of the "City of the Dead" and observes at close range the cemetery's remarkable variety of design.*

but the one in Recoleta is special in many ways. It is the one spot in Buenos Aires where what has been built is strictly respected and where no concessions to modernity—or postmodernity—have been permitted.

Once an orchard for the adjacent convent, the thirteen and a half acres were converted into a public cemetery in 1822. In 1881 Juan Antonio Buschiazzo, the architect who designed and oversaw the creation of the Avenida de Mayo, among other public works, remodeled the cemetery, giving it a Greek-style entrance, set off with Ionic columns.

Visitors have been compelled to describe it ever since. Frances Parkinson Keyes was struck by its location and size: "We wandered through the chapel-bordered stone walks of Recoleta, the cemetery with hundreds of mausolea and monuments and not a single grave. It covers 60,000 square yards in the heart of the city." In 1917 Gordon Ross, then financial editor of *The Standard,* an English-language daily in Buenos Aires, saw the site as "a strange city of the dead in which the coffins are seen on shelves contained in small plate-glass fronted temples, so that all may view the last out-

ward casings of generations." For Koebel, "The Recoleta is known by many as the Westminster Abbey of Buenos Aires. The comparison is not in the least accurate in a physical sense, since the Recoleta, far from being a cathedral, is composed of a collection of many hundreds of chapels and tombs in which the notable dead of Argentina lie. It is a town of the defunct that strangely resembles one of the living. Intersected by parallel stone streets with the tombs for houses on either side, the spectacular effect of the Recoleta is solemn and impressive. The favorite pattern of the chapel itself is Grecian, with a short flight of steps leading to the double entrance doors. Much of the statuary is extremely fine. Perhaps of all the great array there is none that is more striking than a gigantic natural block of marble, from one point on the surface of which has been exquisitely carved the figure of a weeping boy—a life-sized body that is rendered all the more eloquent from the natural stone on which it stands."

As Annie Peck pointed out as long ago as 1913, Recoleta is "a city for the dead among the living, a *crowded* city with no room for more, save in the lots and tombs already well filled." More than eighty years later, the cemetery is still a major sociological and architectural attraction for all visitors to the city, evoking a wide range of reactions. "To be buried in one of these ornate crypts, you must be related to one of Argentina's 'name' families. A general or two in the family tree would also help. The allure of the necropolis is such that even mourners have the air of apartment hunters, doggedly searching out immortality with a view." That is journalist Joseph Hooper's rather irreverent version of how porteños relate to their centrally located cemetery.

Just across the street from the cemetery is one of Buenos Aires's most popular restaurant rows, with more than a dozen prime prospects for

FAR RIGHT *An allegorical scene of angels coming to escort a soul heavenward hovers atop an ornate tomb. This rococo masterpiece of sculptural overkill stands adjacent to a fortresslike tomb of medieval solemnity.*

RIGHT *Eva Perón and her brother Juan Duarte are buried in the Recoleta Cemetery. Three bronze plaques attached to the black marble tomb of the Duarte family commemorate the crucial role the Duarte and Perón families have played in Argentine history.*

LEFT AND RIGHT *Light and shadow play along the streets of tombs at the Recoleta Cemetery. The patriarch of each family dictated the style to be used in building the monumental mausoleum to house his and his descendants' remains. Master sculptors, mostly from Italy, were commissioned by the families to decorate the mausoleums.*

BELOW *A gem of Art Nouveau elegance arises out of the surrounding shadows in the late afternoon light. The delicateness of its sinuous lines, the flowing grace of the angel figure, and the whimsy of the wrought-iron fence that protects the angel make this tomb one of the most appealing of all.*

LEFT AND RIGHT *A melange of funerary art stands guard over the tombs of Buenos Aires's elite.*

a great steak or more elaborate cuisine. No builder dared construct apartment houses overlooking the 6,500 tombs, so since the 1960s the perimeter has gone commercial.

Nearby, one also finds the National Museum of Fine Arts, which was originally a pumping station for the municipal water company, converted into a museum in 1931; the National Exhibition Halls, once home to an ice skating rink; and the Recoleta Cultural Center, a convent in the eighteenth century and now a labyrinthine space for art shows. One major area in which Buenos Aires has lagged behind the rest of the world is the design of museum buildings.

The Recoleta offers something for everyone: street performers, dogs by the dozen leashed to vigorous young walkers, art exhibits galore, a well-stocked design center, places to stare and be stared at, boutiques, a bookshop, hotels, and eateries for every palate and pocketbook. Every porteño engages in some sort of activity in the Recoleta at least once a month. Along with its recent rival, Puerto Madero—the city's newest restaurant row perched

along the waterways of the port—the Recoleta epitomizes upscale, public Buenos Aires today.

Before exploring private Buenos Aires, that sector of the city and its surroundings that has traditionally catered to the ever-changing elite, a question. Why Buenos Aires? Latin America is dotted with cities that seemed, centuries ago, to offer a much brighter future than this precarious port on the Plate.

Why did this unlikely colony at the end of nowhere, ignored by its rulers and execrated by its inhabitants, suddenly blossom in the late nineteenth century into the largest city south of the equator? During the colonial period, the cities that seemed destined to become the metropolises of the future were Mexico City and Lima, with Havana and Recife as contenders. They, too, grew, but were

ABOVE *Café de la Paix, strategically placed at the corner where Avenida Quintana ends and the Recoleta begins, attracts a crowd that wants to look and be looked at.*

OPPOSITE AND LEFT *Not far from the Recoleta Cemetery, the Xul Solar Museum is a recent and welcome addition to the city. Xul invented his own language, a personal system of symbols, and a body of work that fascinated his friend Jorge Luis Borges. The ultra-contemporary building provides a stimulating setting for the small watercolors of Argentina's most inventive artist.*

unable to adapt to the changing times as well as Buenos Aires did.

Buenos Aires had been just an afterthought of the Viceroyalty of Peru, given the token title of Prefecture in 1617. The city finally received recognition in 1776, when the Spanish court named it the seat of an independent viceroyalty, realizing that its situation as a port would be crucial in the future.

The basic city was but 144 blocks square, spreading out from the main plaza, which was the site of a fort, a church, and the governor's adobe "palace," all situated on the perimeter of what today is the Plaza de Mayo. When the city became the seat of the viceroyalty—the same year that the United States declared its independence—the population was only 25,000.

The port, which supplied the city with its chief source of revenue, did not have a decent pier or customs house until 1854. Before that date, getting ashore from a ship was in itself something of an adventure, as an English diplomat, Sir Woodbine Parrish, observed in the 1830s: "Vessels drawing over fifteen or sixteen feet have to drop anchor seven or eight miles off the coast of the city. . . . Nothing could be more inconvenient than the present mode of going ashore. There is rarely enough water to reach the bank in smaller boats and, on approaching it, one is assailed on all sides by carts that drive into the river in search of passengers. Their shape and construction are typical of this country: a base of planks two or three inches apart, through which the water splashes at every wave, mounted on a big, heavy wooden axle between a pair of gigantic wheels. To this ungovernable machine is tied a horse. . . . The wild, brutish appearance of the sun-tanned cart drivers who, half naked, swear and scream and shove at one another and whip their poor

exhausted horses into the water, is sufficient to amaze the foreign visitor arriving there for the first time, and make him doubt that he is indeed landing on Christian soil."

In the hundred years following conferral of viceroyal status—a period that witnessed the twin declarations of independence, the final consolidation of the country, and the naming of Buenos Aires as its capital—the population grew steadily, but there was absolutely no indication of the explosion that was to come. In 1880 the city had 300,000 inhabitants, and just a few years later, its boundaries were stretched to their present configuration.

By 1900, railway lines fanned out in five different directions from Buenos Aires, with the latest-model British rolling stock carrying immigrants into the countryside and returning with agricultural products to be shipped to Europe. The city was equipped with one transport system after another, each of which foreign visitors delighted in calling "the world's best." First came the horse-drawn omnibuses, then electric trams, suburban commuter trains, taxis, and finally 142 bus lines, which crisscross the city in such a way that the system is still considered the world's most convenient.

As the city's structure took shape in the early 1900s, municipal authorities had to contend with

The number 60 bus is one of the city's most ubiquitous. It runs north from the Constitución train station downtown all the way to the delta region known as Tigre and beyond. Buenos Aires offers its residents one of the most highly organized and least expensive public transportation systems in the world.

earlier mistakes or miscalculations to accommodate Buenos Aires's unexpected growth: 300,000 to 3,000,000 in the fifty years from 1880 to 1930. Museum director Alberto Petrina describes the mind-boggling process in an article titled "The Mutating City" in the Italian architectural journal *Abitare*. "Almost nothing remains of the original city: the stump of the Cabildo, Viceroy Liniers' house on Calle Venezuela and the Pilar Church. The original city beat to the rhythm of two hearts— one urban (the plaza), the other architectural (the patio)—which organized the entire structure in a truly intelligent way. The grid layout imposed not just a concept of utopia, but also rationality, the 'dream of order' that Europe had never known or had never wanted to create for itself, but had willingly transferred to America."

Italian immigration, which outnumbered all other, even Spanish, supplied the city with skilled builders and artisans, and gave the city a new face, that of master masons' stucco facades, decorated with their quirky angelic faces and mythological beauty-contest bodies. Petrina continues, "By around 1890, Italianate academicism was the dominant style everywhere. The houses of the old Barrio Sur, which Borges later described with such melancholy, and the front facade of the Casa Rosada and the Church of the Immaculate Conception in Belgrano are the outstanding stylistic achievements of this period. The magnificent Colón Theater stands as a model of the changes implicitly wrought by French academicism, the city's next stylistic metamorphosis. Though the building is still Italianate on the outside, the foyer and theater itself have all the triumphal sumptuousness of the Beaux-Arts style. Under the city's first mayor, Torcuato de Alvear, the city espoused Haussmann's principles of urban design and committed itself once and for all to a fully cosmopolitan identity."

Local architects kept incorporating new ideas from Europe. Art Nouveau took on a local flavor, as did Art Deco when its turn came. "In the early 1930s, the city learned a new architectural language that would finally make it an authentic modern metropolis. The Modern movement came and stayed, first in its German and New York versions, and then in the guise of Le Corbusier. White returned to the streets, but this time as a symbol of the new, unadorned, nautical style. Sometimes,

A set of ornate balconies with an inverted bow window crowned by a pair of playful cherubs is one of the city's more fanciful facades. Magnificent wrought-iron grillwork and excellent carpentry make this building a masterpiece of early-twentieth-century urban design.

TOP RIGHT *The fanciful main entrance to the Argentine Yacht Club looks out on the Telecom Building and the city beyond.*

BOTTOM RIGHT *A life preserver is vividly inscribed with the club's flag and insignia. The emerging sun with arched brows is also found on the country's flag.*

BELOW *The Art Deco tower of the Argentine Yacht Club is a landmark for all passengers plying the River Plate to and from Uruguay.*

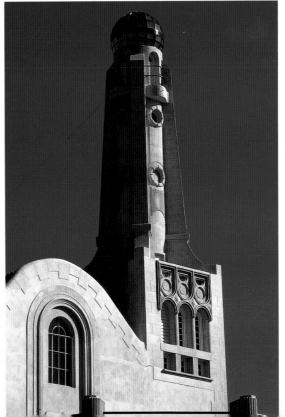

OPPOSITE *Standing sentinel at the mouth of the city's harbor, the Argentine Yacht Club, designed by architect Edouard Le Monnier, is exuberantly Art Deco. Most of the members prefer to moor their sailboats at the club's larger headquarters in San Fernando.*

ABOVE *A view of the Argentine Yacht Club from the deck of a ship in the harbor. Once the main entrance to the port, this basin now handles hydrofoils offering service across the river to Uruguay.*

BELOW *Set on a triangular lot facing Plaza San Martín, the Kavanagh Building was the city's first skyscraper. Built in 1934–35, the 33-story building is 350 feet tall and was designed in part to provide a pied-à-terre in town for visiting estancieros.*

RIGHT *Looking down from a terrace atop the Kavanagh Building, one can get an idea of what rush hour traffic is like in Buenos Aires.*

as with the Kavanagh, South America's finest modernist building, gun-metal gray gave it the appearance of the prow of a futurist battleship. The new functionalist architecture coexisted harmoniously with the French style, leaving its unmistakable mark on an area as large as Barrio Norte," Petrina observed.

Modernism's white facades, austere silhouettes, and harmonious lines spread throughout the city. A new mentality was forming in Argentina, and local architects were incorporating it and interpreting it in their designs. "The boom in Modernism was more a matter of satisfying the needs of a new middle class growing steadily thanks to a relatively stable economy and currency that were nurturing the country's nascent manufacturing industries, which in turn were attracting a stream of immigrants from the interior of the country to the city. The new industrial mentality quickly exposed the shortcomings of the building techniques that academic architectural design both implied and

ABOVE *A desk in Roberto Devorik's apartment in the Kavanagh Building features a small replica of the Eiffel Tower and three obelisks. Photos of Mr. Devorik in the company of his close friend Princess Diana have pride of place. A turn-of-the-century French painting sets the tone.*

ABOVE *A touch of India is the motif in the Devorik study. The handsomely framed watercolor of an elephant and driver is repeated in the design of the pillows below. Trompe-l'oeil bookshelves cover the walls.*

LEFT *With its sumptuous curtains, warm yellow walls, handsome mirror, French School painting, Oriental objects, and comfortable couch, the Devorik living room is a perfect example of the refinement in taste to be found in Buenos Aires.*

entailed. Architects who had previously worked in a wide range of styles began simplifying classical models, rationalizing building materials, and eliminating everything that might prove an obstacle to production-line construction techniques," architect Marcelo Barreiro points out in his article "La Modernitá Conveniente" (low-cost modernism) in *Abitare*.

From the 1940s on, the story is a less felicitous one. One of the most disturbing results of the post–World War II building boom in Buenos Aires was the proliferation of *medianeras*—multistory solid cement walls that stand on property lines, towering over smaller century-old buildings. The city's ever-changing and erratically enforced building code is to blame for these obtrusive structures. Decades may pass before buildings of similar height rise to hide this aberration of the urban landscape.

The evolution of the city from its Spanish and Italian periods, through the decorative French phase, to the functionalism of the 1940s and the budget-conscious, cost-cutting pragmatism of the 1960s and onward has changed the city's character, and this transformation has also been reflected in the inhabitants' lifestyle. One renegade architect, Rodolfo Livingston, possessed of a wicked sense of humor and an acute dose of humanism, has written a book titled *Cirugia de Casas* (Surgery on houses; 1990), in which he offers the average homeowner a series of tips on how to beat the system. One is to cut your own windows into the soulless expanse of a *medianera*, thereby gaining more light and a better view until the unlikely arrival of a neighboring building.

A recent initiative that has brightened the city is the recruitment of private sponsors to maintain the city's parks and plazas. The municipal government's hiring and firing policies had become so distorted that there were more barbers on the Public Works Department's payroll than gardeners. Now, with the outrageous exception of the large plaza in front of Congress, most of Buenos Aires's principal green spaces look green again.

One anomaly to the city's green-space policy is a vast area of unused land along the river, just behind the Casa Rosada. Le Corbusier, who came to the city to deliver a series of lectures in 1929, envisioned "a large plateau built out over the river with restaurants, cafés, and all the places people need to relax in, where the citizens of Buenos Aires will at last have regained the right to see the sea and the sky." Fulvio Inace, in citing Le Corbusier in *Abitare*, adds that the French architect's project was inspired by the sea, the immense port, and the magnificent vegetation of the parks in Palermo.

Le Corbusier's idea was never adopted, nor was the proposal for an island airport just off the city's coastline by Amancio Williams, Buenos Aires's most creative conceptual architect. A version of the project is now under discussion, however, along with a twenty-five-mile-long bridge across the

Enthusiastic art students paint historically or politically inspired murals on the medianeras, *the walls that are revealed when adjacent buildings are torn down or multistory buildings go up next to older, lower structures. This wall, in San Telmo, was denuded when Avenida Independencia was widened.*

River Plate to Uruguay, which would provide a more direct overland connection with southern Brazil and eventually São Paulo.

The promenades along what were once the banks of the River Plate, stretching both north and south from the downtown port area, where access to the river had been sacrificed for the construction of a commercial seaport, were also to lose their direct access to the river.

For years these promenades, built around the turn of the century and known as the Costanera Norte and the Costanera Sur, offered fishermen a

chance to catch a fresh meal and marginal restaurateurs to sell steaks from precarious carts. As time passed and more porteños acquired cars, the carts grew in size and complexity.

The city finally decided to tidy up the area and in an overnight military-style operation demolished all the carts, replacing them with concessioned restaurants boasting both running water and bathrooms. In the post–World War II period, as Buenos Aires adapted to the lifestyles of the rest of the Western world, many of the old palatial homes were demolished, and the rubble became landfill. On the north-

LEFT *This romantic view is deceptive; the Ecological Reserve is a landfill that nature has temporarily reclaimed but that man has managed to leave virtually abandoned.*

ABOVE *A sunny afternoon brings hordes of sunbathers to the green areas of the Costanera Sur on weekends. Flowering trees provide the city with a colorful backdrop for much of the year.*

RIGHT *Riders of this motorcycle built for three relax along the wall that marks the frontier of the Ecological Reserve, the landfill taken over by hearty vegetation and wildlife. Motorcycles have staged a remarkable comeback in Buenos Aires in recent years.*

ern side of the port, where the downtown airport provides a buffer against housing projects, the land-fill, which has deprived fishermen and bathers of easy access, has been dedicated to gas stations, a golf driving range, night clubs, and entertainment complexes. The turn-of-the-century Fishing Club, with its long, narrow pier, still stands as a lonely sentinel penetrating a hundred yards into the Plate.

On the southern side, the resulting 865-acre weed patch—awarded the politically correct name

of Ecological Reserve—became a political foot-ball, coveted by conservationists and real estate developers alike.

The Ecological Reserve is a polder that was accidentally saved from development by the con-flicting legislation governing the reclaimed strip of land. Declared a natural park in the 1980s, the area

It took Buenos Aires centuries to build a port. Now Puerto Madero, part of the old port area, is home to elegant restaurants and lofts that look across this channel at an obsolete grain storage facility. The large sailing ship was once a Navy training vessel for midshipmen.

now boasts a few trees—mostly willows and ceibos *(Erythrina crista-galli)*, and is home to the city's only wild nutrias, flamingos, egrets, ducks, and parrots. Unfortunately, the reserve's future is uncertain; the area is strangely prone to brush fires, and commercial real estate schemes are a constant menace. In any case, should imagination and intelligence win out, today's controversial and derelict Ecological Reserve may give Buenos Aires a breath of fresh life in the twenty-first century.

Although Le Corbusier's riverfront project was never implemented, a modified version, combining a business center with a recreational space, is being realized. The government privatized sixteen warehouses in the port area along the edge of the downtown area. International and local investors converted these striking brick structures into lofts, offices, and restaurants, giving city dwellers a chance to stroll from the city's center to the water's edge for the first time in recent history.

Puerto Madero—the development is named for the section of the port where it is located—covers 420 acres. A hundred are destined for commercial development, 80 for public spaces, 94 for waterways, and the remainder await future development. The development plan—initiated in 1989—was the ninth idea to be offered the city in the last half century.

The city, in reality, has three possible alternatives for expansion: (1) continuing its relentless march inland and sending its workers—executives and laborers alike—to sleep along its edge in the Province of Buenos Aires; (2) expanding atop the river, on landfills and/or man-made islands; and (3) jumping across the River Plate to the Uruguayan coast, and commuting by hydrofoil and, eventually, bus or car.

The irresistible magnet that has already attracted more than 30 percent of Argentina's population—

both from abroad and from the interior—to settle in the metropolitan area will continue to lure millions more in coming decades, creating the need for brave new solutions to resolve the deficit in homes and land on which to build them.

What the next twist in architecture will be is impossible to foretell. It will, of necessity, have to be inexpensive, easy to finance, and more humane than recent attempts at large-scale housing. It will also have to be connected by efficient rapid-transit systems to and from the workplace. These changes, too, will continue to erode the classic porteño lifestyle, even though the city's nostalgia-producing infrastructure continues to exist and, in certain cases, flourish.

ABOVE *The old brick customs warehouses in Puerto Madero, now converted into lofts and offices, offer ground-floor dining with a view of the harbor.*

OPPOSITE *A modern hovercraft, the renovated customs warehouse complex, and a state-of-the-art office building designed by Cesar Pelli are the highlights along this stretch of coast in downtown Buenos Aires.*

CHAPTER 4

Private Buenos Aires

In spite of changes in government, financial crises, debt debacles, and constant general confusion, many a porteño continues to keep his lifestyle basically intact and his home an inviolate castle. The city's residential areas hug the hundred or so blocks of Avenida del Libertador, which originates downtown at the Retiro Station on the corner of Plaza San Martín and ends twenty-five miles north, near Tigre, where the delta of the Paraná River is divided into dozens of islands.

The porteño's image of the ideal home has changed radically since the beginning of the century, as has the neighborhood in which he would like to live. The city's most favored residential areas have gradually shifted northward, and the dependence on French styles has given way to more international expressions of contemporary architecture. The palatial homes of the city's golden age have now passed into institutional hands. No one would consider building a French *grand hôtel* today; nor would anyone think to build a sumptuous home downtown.

An occasional magnate of the moment might put a helicopter pad atop a garage roof in the city itself, but most self-made moguls prefer a larger piece of land to build what is apt to be Californian

Greek Revival is but one of the diverse styles of residential architecture to be found in Buenos Aires.

LEFT *Inventor of his own artistic style, which he calls Railway Art, Carlos Regazzoni has painted the murals that grace the Retiro Station in downtown Buenos Aires, where he lives when not working in his Paris studio.*

RIGHT *Regazzoni's "bedroom" in a vast old warehouse at the Retiro Station is packed with his creations: paintings, graphic works, objects, and sculptures made from remnants of Argentine railways.*

BELOW *The director of the freight division of the Mitre Railway lent Reggazoni the huge warehouse several years ago. The artist moved in, and it is here that he paints, sculpts, prepares* asados, *and sells examples of his unique Railway Art.*

RIGHT *The Grill at the once traditional Plaza Hotel, now the Marriott Plaza, has been a favorite of the Argentine aristocracy since a wealthy banking family opened the strategically located hotel in 1908. A post-adolescent Aristotle Onassis got his first tips here as a telephone operator.*

OPPOSITE, TOP *The Plaza Hotel, at the edge of Plaza San Martín, is overshadowed by the Kavanagh Building, once the city's tallest skyscraper.*

OPPOSITE, BOTTOM
Presiding over Plaza San Martín is the magnificent monument to General José de San Martín, Liberator of Argentina and several neighboring republics. The first sculpture in Argentina to portray a hero on horseback, the large bronze was created by French artist Louis-Joseph Daumas over a century ago. The ornate base was added several decades later.

in context rather than Parisian in appearance. Yet the palatial homes that still grace the downtown area are what give the city its touch of class.

Those porteños who can afford to, live along an axis parallel to the river—never directly on the muddy water of the River Plate itself. The coastline is now a mix of parking lots for containers, sand deposits, gas stations, restaurants, an airport, and an occasional club. A highway and a rail line separate the city from its waterfront. The parks in Palermo provide a wide green buffer, making a wonderful foreground for residents of the high-rise apartments that stretch along Avenida del Libertador from Retiro well into the nearby northern suburbs.

Skyscrapers with a river view or facing a park or a plaza command a premium, as do houses on a broad, tree-lined avenue in a quieter neighborhood such as the one surrounding the Belgrano R train station. Better cars, better highways, and better security have caused an exodus to patrolled, self-contained garden communities within an hour and a half of downtown. Fortunately, this flight from the city, and even from its adjacent suburbs, has not yet affected the quality or style of life in the city itself.

At the turn of the century, the city's wealthiest landed families built mansions on as grandiose a scale as ever seen anywhere. Today these still spec-tacular buildings house embassies or institutions and remain a well-tended reminder of the elegance and refinement that characterized the city a century ago.

By 1900 the city's center of gravity had moved north from the Plaza de Mayo area toward Barrio Norte and Recoleta. The grand homes of the early decades of the twentieth century were built around the Plaza San Martín, the Plazoleta Carlos Pellegrini, and along the five blocks of Avenida Alvear that con-nect the Plazoleta Carlos Pellegrini with Recoleta.

The first and grandest of these extravagant residences (Plaza San Martín) was the palace built

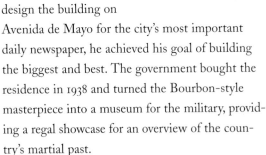

by José C. Paz, founder of *La Prensa.* In 1909 Paz commissioned French architect Louis Sortais to design the imposing building and, as he had done when he commissioned Parisian architects in 1902 to design the building on Avenida de Mayo for the city's most important daily newspaper, he achieved his goal of building the biggest and best. The government bought the residence in 1938 and turned the Bourbon-style masterpiece into a museum for the military, providing a regal showcase for an overview of the country's martial past.

Jorge Luis Borges lived just across the street, on the sixth floor of a nondescript rationalist-style apartment house (Maipú 994). Borges's lifestyle was a simple one. After a brief first marriage he lived with his mother, and after her death, with a maid and a cat. When he married María Kodama, the couple settled in Geneva until his death. The Buenos Aires apartment had two bedrooms and a living-dining room. The walls were covered with artwork, mostly gifts from friends and admirers. Bookcases contained his favorite works, which he could quickly locate in spite of his blindness. The perennial Nobel Prize candidate would receive his guests seated on a well-worn couch, his cane close at hand, ready to go out for a meal around the corner at the Norte Restaurant, his favorite neighborhood haunt.

Across the Plaza San Martín, the Anchorena family built a three-part complex (Arenales 761),

joined by a *cour d'honneur* in the best eighteenth-century French style. The building, designed by Alejandro Christophersen, won the Municipal Prize of 1910. The Ministry of Foreign Relations moved into the residence in 1936.

With each passing decade, the construction of grand homes shifted northward. In 1921 architect Martín Noel built his own exotic Neocolonial home (Suipacha 1420). Founder of a movement called Colonial Renaissance, Noel abandoned all dependence on the French model and sought his inspiration in Spanish colonial and American indigenous design. This unique contribution to the city's seigneurial residences, with its staggered patios and extensive gardens, is now the city's Museum of Spanish-American Art.

At this time the Plazoleta Carlos Pellegrini and Avenida Alvear in Barrio Norte provided

The Isaac Fernández Blanco Museum of Spanish-American Art is housed in the Neocolonial residence that architect Martín Noel designed for himself in 1921. In addition to the museum's excellent collection of colonial silver and religious art, it has wonderful gardens.

Celedonio Pereda's marvelous mansion, featuring ceilings painted by José María Sert, is now the residence of the Brazilian ambassador. The palatial home overlooks the Plazoleta Carlos Pellegrini and is fortunately maintained to perfection by its current occupants.

Argentina's most powerful ranchers *(estancieros)* with virgin sites for their urban residences, consolidating the city's progressive shift northward. In 1917 the influential rancher Celedonio Pereda commissioned French architect Louis Martin to design a mansion that would define the owner's privileged position in porteño society. Pereda wanted a replica of the Jacquemart-André Museum in Paris. Jules Dormal, on finishing the construction of the Colón Theater, was called in to adapt the original plan and supervise the building of

the monumental home, which the Pereda family moved into in 1924. In 1932 José María Sert, the Spanish artist, decorated the palace's ceilings with wonderful allegorical murals, which can still be enjoyed today.

On nearby Cerrito Street, set on such a strategic site that the city had to bend the broad Nueve de Julio Avenue around it, the Ortiz Basualdo family commissioned French architect Paul Pater in 1913 to create a *grand hôtel* of striking design and dimensions (Cerrito 1390). The result was a recycled

gem of French architecture that is now, appropriately, the home of the French Embassy.

Across the street and down one of the city's few hills the Alzaga Unzué Palace (Cerrito 1433), designed in 1916 by Robert Prentice, along with the Atucha Palace (Arroyo 1099), designed by René Sergent in 1924, rounded out the French-style residences at the Plazoleta. The Alzaga Unzué home was recently saved from the wrecker by the clamor of impassioned neighbors. Instead of destroying the beautiful building, the Hyatt Hotel found itself making the felicitous decision to restore it and incorporate it into the hotel's gardens. The Atucha Palace is the only one still remaining in private hands.

Heading toward Recoleta along Avenida Alvear, the Duhau (Alvear 1683) and Fernández Anchorena (Alvear 1637) residences provide two more examples of the French *grand hôtel* style. Both were built on plots of land that stretch from Alvear down the hillside to Posadas Street. The Fernández Anchorena Palace, designed by French architect Edouard Le Monnier and inaugurated in 1909, is now the home of the Papal Nuncio.

As in New York, and to a certain extent Paris, most of these historic homes changed owners, often ending up in unexpected hands. The military, the Vatican, the French, the Brazilians, the Hyatt Hotel chain, and the Foreign Ministry now all struggle to maintain these massive monuments to the city's glorious past, without recourse to the regiments of trained and dedicated servants who put maintenance before indolence for the greater glory of the Anchorena and the Paz families.

While the *grand hôtel* style was limited to the superrich, *petits hôtels* sprang up like mushrooms around the opulent mansions of Barrio Norte. Here wealthy merchants, doctors, and lawyers raised their large families with the faithful support of a dozen or so servants. As their myriad children grew and set

out on their own, equally elegant apartment houses were built for their comfort. Often a *petit hôtel* owner's flock of offspring would be given an entire apartment building to house their own growing families. These apartments would occupy an entire floor, with half a dozen bedrooms and a similar number of rooms for the staff.

By 1930 modern architectural styles took precedence over French models, and more and more ten- to fifteen-story apartment buildings were built as rental properties. Gone were Parisian stone facades and mansard roofs. Many of the new buildings were derived from what was locally called the yacht style, with curved chrome railings on balconies, flat masonry walls, and Art Deco–like angles.

Historic masterpieces featuring Ionic, Doric, and Corinthian columns borrowed from Greece, as well as Renaissance, Baroque, Neo-Gothic, Moorish, Byzantine, Neocolonial, Egyptian, and even

In 1913 the Ortiz Basualdo family asked French architect Paul Pater to design this grand home. Fittingly, it now serves as the French Embassy. The city's main thoroughfare, Avenida 9 de Julio, was rerouted around the building to save it from demolition.

LEFT *Plaza Lavalle is home to a motley assortment of buildings, including a glass tower and a Neoclassical structure topped by an ornate cupola. General Lavalle himself stands atop a tall pillar, built to protect him from damage by ardent enemies of his memory.*

OPPOSITE, TOP *The Cervantes National Theater was built in 1921 by a troupe of Spanish actors and taken over by the State in 1926 when the theatrical company went bankrupt. Built in the Spanish Neo-Plateresque style, the theater was recently renovated.*

OPPOSITE, BOTTOM *One of the few contemporary bank buildings in the city was designed by architects Mario Botta and Haig Uluhogian in 1988 for the Banca Nazionale del Lavoro. Across Diagonal Norte, the baroque cupola of the Bencich Building (1927) provides a striking contrast.*

Hindu and Assyrian details, all inspired architects to look deeper into history for inspiration in their quest to change the face of the city to one less dependent on classical French design.

The expanding middle class began to share these buildings with descendants of the landed aristocracy. Eyes turned from French decor toward innovative styles originating elsewhere in Europe and in the United States.

Less space meant fewer servants, and the previously opulent lifestyle was replaced by a more austere one. The external wooden shutters usually stayed closed to protect the curtains from the intrusive sunlight. Living room furniture was often draped in

flowing white cloth to keep the dust off and the light from fading the upholstery. Family life moved closer to the kitchen, and entertainment on a grand scale became a practice reserved for holidays.

Another victim of the reduction in staff was the family dog. Once able to romp in the family's private garden, later escorted around the block several times a day by an obliging minion, and finally walked by reluctant children, most dogs now get their exercise in the company of a dozen of their peers, led by dog walkers who guide their packs to the park for a couple of hours each day.

True dog lovers, overwhelmed by this disintegration of the traditional urban amenities, have moved to the suburbs, where pets and children can be unleashed in the garden. The most common discussion at dinners these days, besides the eternal lament about servants' behavior and cost, is whether one should move north and escape the increasingly unpleasant realities of downtown urban existence. So many have already left that now a majority of

BELOW AND RIGHT Dog walkers escort their charges for several hours every day. The dogs learn to be among the most disciplined pedestrians in Buenos Aires. Small ones scamper to keep up with their larger companions until they reach a park where they can romp at their ease.

the city's economically comfortable citizens live beyond Belgrano, where the grass is greener and the building lots are larger.

Although Buenos Aires still has a homeowner/servant ratio that is higher than anywhere west of Asia, each successive generation has had to cope with providing for more and more of its personal needs. Country club life, which flourishes, offers a respite on weekends, as do trips to country homes in the suburbs or on estancias. Porteños are known throughout the world as enthusiastic, almost obsessive shoppers. Affluent families tend to make two major international trips a year—one to Europe and another to Miami or the Caribbean. Those with lesser resources delight in Chile or Brazil.

As one moves northward, each neighborhood caters to a different mind-set. If Barrio Norte, Recoleta, and Barrio Parque contain the descendants of once-distinguished families, and Palermo boasts

a less formal kind of lifestyle, as well as Villa Freud, where the world's greatest concentration of analysts tends hordes of neurotic city dwellers, Belgrano is basically a yuppy enclave, where cars, square meters, and dress codes mark your place in the local pecking order. Once beyond Belgrano, however, residents relax, and it is not until you get to San Isidro some fifteen miles north that an open awareness of caste and clan consciousness takes over again.

If a symmetrical academicism and a respect for the laws of composition predominated in the residential architecture that appeared from the 1930s to the 1950s, the 1960s saw a sad switch to buildings engineered as cheaply as possible. This sacrifice of style and elegance brought a dramatic change to the city's skyline. Almost every city block is marred by those immense *medianeras*—occasionally made even more ugly by glaring advertising murals. This constant assault on the eye is the most distressing reality of the rape of the city's once harmonious horizon.

A plethora of garish signs confuses the pedestrian, who has to adapt his vision to McDonald's red and yellow, the phone company's blue and green, and myriad less recognizable but equally aggressive color combinations. Noisy and noxious buses and mosquitolike motorcycles damage the eardrum and attack the lungs. But compared to other cities of similar size and relevance, Buenos Aires remains something of a paradise, where a visitor can circulate at any hour, bask in the shade of millions of trees, and enjoy street corner cafés, colorful flower and fruit stalls, and rambling streetside magazine stands, all in the company of well-groomed passersby and beneath a brilliant sun that shines more days a year than in any comparable city in the northern hemisphere.

Once you enter the city's homes, anything goes, as long as it is designed to imitate a shelter maga-

Casa Leonor caters to the still-thriving community of uniformed domestic personnel. Neatly dressed maids continue to be an integral part of upper-middle-class everyday life in Buenos Aires.

LEFT *A corner produce shop in the charming Palermo Viejo neighborhood offers specials on grapefruit, eggs, and tomatoes. Shopkeepers and residents are just beginning to realize that their ornately decorated turn-of-the-century facades are worth restoring and highlighting.*

ABOVE *La Esquina de las Flores (The Corner of the Flowers) is one of the city's busiest health-food centers. Its postmodern Art Nouveau decor adds a bit of color to an otherwise shabby downtown neighborhood.*

RIGHT *The Bar Taller in Palermo Viejo is a place to get a good burger during the day and listen to hot music at night. The graffiti-style bicycle on its facade is an unusual sight in Buenos Aires.*

LEFT *A patchwork of boxes of color-ful fruits and vegetables entices the passerby in Palermo Viejo. Red watermelon and ripe peaches indicate that it is January in Buenos Aires.*

ABOVE *On the eve of any national holiday, vendors fill the sidewalks with souvenirs sporting the Argentine national colors. They come in all shapes and sizes, from regulation flags to tiny bows to pin on the lapel. The badges displayed on the sides of this stand are the shields of major soccer teams.*

ABOVE AND LEFT *El Gato Negro (the Black Cat) is Buenos Aires's leading purveyor of spices, tea, and coffee. Shopping here has been a tradition among gourmets for decades. The mascot himself poses in front of bins of coffee that display painted versions of him wearing different colored bows (above). He also controls traffic on Avenida Corrientes from his perch on the ledge in front of the specialty shop (left).*

OPPOSITE *Clasica y Moderna is that rare combination of a bookstore with a bar/restaurant. It also offers art exhibits, piano recitals, and jazz.*

ABOVE *What a neighborhood café lacks in atmosphere, it makes up for with hearty food and affable patrons.*

RIGHT AND BELOW *The Café Ideal is one of the last of the grand cafés that used to flourish throughout the center of the city. It struggles to* maintain *its fading dignity in the face of proliferating fast-food emporiums. A veteran bartender mixes a Negroni on a copper counter (below). The hardwood, compartmentalized refrigerator behind him is a reminder that the Ideal has been a popular place to learn and dance the tango since 1920.*

The Edelweiss Restaurant, just off
Avenida Corrientes and a block from
the Obelisk, caters to the theatrical
world. Seated at the far right is
Enrique Pinti, a political comedian
whose everchanging one-man show has
commanded a full house for decades.

zine illustration. Porteños are very correct in their attitude toward decor. Few have strayed from European standards set a hundred years ago. While some still have family collections that deserve this gilded-age treatment, most depend on reproduction furniture and late editions of period engravings to re-create a pseudo-European flavor. A flair for the unexpected is finally starting to appear, although a

certain stiffness, a lack of whimsy, perhaps, is more characteristic of porteño homes.

Decades of visits to Villa Freud may have helped loosen up local taste patterns, but a dependency on the tried and true leaves little room for the innovative, no less the outré. Still, five thousand artists, hundreds of decorators, and countless antiques shops manage to survive in Buenos Aires.

As the city moves closer to the world it admires, customs and manners are changing. And, as a revival of self-confidence sweeps the city, a more personal approach toward decorating can be anticipated.

Las Violetas, in the distant neighbor-hood of Flores, is a café that evokes nostalgia for the past. Its coffee and croissants make it a popular Sunday morning destination.

ABOVE *Rafael de Oliveira Cézar's world-class Art Deco collection includes this Jean Dunand gilt and lacquered wooden screen and a Eugene Printz chair.*

LEFT *His sitting room overlooks busy Avenida 9 de Julio. Trompe l'oeil murals cover walls and ceiling. An early-twentieth-century table and chair by Rembrandt Bugatti and an Art Deco rug by Ivan da Silva Bruhns mix with a Louis XV chandelier.*

OPPOSITE *Drawings, engravings, photos, and paintings of thoroughbred horses cover the walls of the study.*

RIGHT *"Dudu" von Thielmann's home on Calle Montevideo in Barrio Norte reflects her passion for collecting. Nothing seems to have escaped her avid eye as she wanders around the globe. On her terrace, metal alligators by Carlos Regazzoni combine with bamboo furniture from the Philippines to produce a bizarre marriage of cult and culture.*

ABOVE *A stone head of the Buddha from Cambodia, a ceramic bull from Peru, a drum from Oceania, and a painting by Argentine artist Cuello surround a mahogany chest from the southern Philippines in Dudu's exuberant penthouse overlooking the gardens of the papal nuncio's residence.*

LEFT *A large abstract painting by Argentine artist Antonio Segui hangs above a selection of Asian objects in a comfortably appointed living room in Barrio Norte.*

BELOW *A green column representing the trunk of a palo borracho tree by contemporary artist Nicolás García Uriburu, a guanaco fur throw, and a potpourri of Argentine and Uruguayan paintings and drawings share the intensely decorated living room in apparent harmony.*

FAR LEFT *A lush wall of greenery with an ornate wrought-iron grill and a classical figure of a flute player set among brightly colored flowers make Puppe Mandl's Barrio Norte garden an oasis just meters from the intersection of two of the city's busiest avenues.*

LEFT *Crafted in Bolivia in the nineteenth century, these sharply pointed silver objects were used by women in the highlands to hold their ponchos in place.*

BELOW *Puppe Mandl's extensive collection of Colonial Spanish-American painting includes fine examples of religious works from Mexico, Bolivia, Peru, and Ecuador mounted in intricately carved and gilded frames.*

OPPOSITE *Four fanlike rice-paper scrolls, inscribed in Chinese and framed in natural wood, add a delicate Oriental charm to the cozy bedroom in decorator Delia Tedin's home near the heart of the city.*

LEFT *Set in a two-block-long passageway, the eighty-year-old house has a patio with a small fountain. Ferns and vines thrive in the yellow-walled microclimate. Double doors, rimmed by tall wooden shutters, lead to a glass-covered alcove.*

ABOVE *An Oriental-looking bird cage shares a table with a fishbowl of lilies from the pond in the patio. In the background, a chair has been upholstered in cloth painted by Gonzalo Gorostiaga.*

OPPOSITE *An indoor swimming pool bathed in natural light and graced with giant ferns creates a semitropical flavor in antiquarian Eduardo Cohen's Barrio Norte home. An extravagant chandelier counterbalances the hanging greenery, and a table set with ivory and bronze sculptures serves as a reminder that we are in the home of a major collector.*

ABOVE *The exquisite curves of the ivory and bronze figures are echoed in those of the orchids that thrive in this hothouse atmosphere, unique in Buenos Aires.*

ABOVE *Eduardo Cohen's bamboo four-poster, surrounded by pieces of his collection of Oriental art, is strategically positioned to overlook the indoor pool.*

LEFT *The countless objects of rare beauty in Eduardo Cohen's home include a towering mantelpiece adorned with ancient Chinese ceramic figures.*

ABOVE *In the home of Adolfo Blaquier Unzué an army of European bronzes stands before a vibrant wallpaper adorned with parrots. A nineteenth-century Italian painting adds to the colorful decor.*

RIGHT *A flamboyant Sèvres urn mounted on an ornate bronze base by master bronze maker Pierre Gouthière is just one of the many fine antiques in the Blaquier Unzué home.*

OPPOSITE *A pair of sixteenth-century French columns flank the entrance to the formal living room, which is appointed with eighteenth-century furniture. The room's high ceiling and pilasters date from an epoch when craftsmen in Buenos Aires could echo French style to perfection.*

LEFT *A bold still life by Perez Becerra provides a strong focal point in Folco and Carolina Landini's minimalist kitchen.*

BELOW *The beautifully designed doors and inlaid stone floor of the entrance open onto a delightful wooden elevator car set in an open shaft with wrought-iron trim, around which curves a marble staircase.*

OPPOSITE *The dining room is another austere space in which paintings from the Landini collection are the protagonists. A large bowl by Juan José Cambre dominates the wall behind the handsome table and elegantly simple set of chairs.*

BELOW *Austere simplicity characterizes the Landini bedroom suite. Paintings, such as Davide Pizzigoni's figure of a young man in the foreground, provide the proper dose of color to the harmonious setting in this Barrio Norte apartment.*

ABOVE *White-and-gray Italian marble lends
architect and interior designer Gonzalo Bruno
Quijano's bath the air of a Roman villa. A neoclassical bronze bench and the shampoo bottles
above the window bring us closer to today.*

LEFT *The highlight of Quijano's sumptuously
decorated Barrio Norte apartment is an eight-
section eighteenth-century Chinese Coromandel
screen depicting a nursery school.*

RIGHT *Another Coromandel screen, this one
depicting a battle scene, serves as the backdrop for
a Louis XVI table and a Louis XV chair. Chinese
porcelain objects complete the decor of this corner of
Quijano's apartment.*

RIGHT *The brick walls and high ceilings of the Palacio Alcorta—a renovated military installation—provide an apt setting for a modern kitchen.*

ABOVE *A simple Oriental screen inscribed with flowing calligraphy separates the living room from an adjacent work space.*

LEFT *Originally a military installation and then a Chrysler plant, the Palacio Alcorta now offers loftlike apartments to affluent city dwellers. The long, narrow pool provides residents with a refreshing view, a rarity in this area of downtown Buenos Aires.*

ABOVE *Industrial lighting fixtures, a cement staircase, and modern furniture impart a minimalist chic to this apartment.*

146   *Private Buenos Aires*

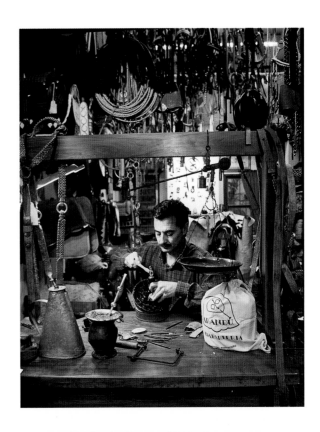

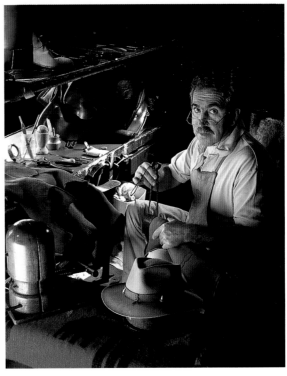

ABOVE *Guillermo Kuitca,
Argentina's most internationally
renowned painter, poses before two of
his recent large canvases. A veteran of
one-man shows at the Museum of
Modern Art in New York and other
major museums, he lives and works in
a rambling house in Belgrano.*

OPPOSITE *Diplomat/author Abel
Posse, now ambassador to Peru, sits
before a bright yellow precursor to the
PC, crafting texts much as a composer
creates a symphony.*

TOP RIGHT *Artisan Norberto Payan
works on a silver bowl in the workshop
of Talabartería Arandú, a family firm of
silversmiths and leather craftsmen dedicated to producing and marketing traditional articles for Argentine ranchers.*

BOTTOM RIGHT *Don Pablo, the
proprietor of Guido, continues a family
tradition that dates back to making boots
for Leonardo Da Vinci. Today, in addition to footwear, Don Pablo specializes
in designing and producing* criollo *sil-
verware and rawhide accessories.*

OPPOSITE *An alcove in artist Nicolás García Uriburu's kitchen is covered from wall to wall and from floor to ceiling with painted wooden masks carved by the Chanes, one of the last remaining indigenous groups in Argentina.*

BELOW *An antique colonial table provides a platform for a large silver crescent, a symbolic ornament that accompanies colonial figures of the Virgin; a variety of sacred figures; and colonial household objects in silver from Spanish settlements in the Andes.*

ABOVE *A founding father of the enviromentalist movement, Uriburu early on colored some of the world's most significant bodies of water as an ecological protest. Here he poses in front of one of his works.*

ABOVE *These colorful rugs and bedspreads in floral and stylized zoomorphic designs are made by descendants of Argentina's original indigenous inhabitants at Ricardo Paz Bullrich's Palermo Viejo headquarters.*

RIGHT *Ricardo Paz Bullrich, descendant of two of Argentina's most traditional families, is a pioneer in reestablishing the carving and weaving arts in northern Argentina.*

FAR RIGHT *This rustic warehouse serves as storage space, restoration lab, and showcase for the country furniture that Ricardo Paz Bullrich gathers, refurbishes, and sells to city folk avid to re-create a rural atmosphere in their urban homes.*

OPPOSITE *Audacious color and eclectic design mark the Palermo Viejo home of Alan Faena, the young founder of Buenos Aires's most outrageous fashion chain. On the terrace, exuberantly colored and patterned pillows piled on an iron chaise create a comfy perch overlooking the sheltered garden.*

BELOW *More elegant than most people's living rooms, the bathroom exemplifies the spirit in which the young fashion mogul has chosen to live. Faena balances an ornate chandelier with a classical chaise longue and allows the vibrant color of the adjacent room to shine in through three square portholes.*

ABOVE *In an otherwise traditional country kitchen, color provides the Faena trademark.*

After the turn of the century, an active and increasingly prosperous middle class developed in Argentina, and along with the elite, they settled in the suburbs of Buenos Aires, where they created an eclectic variety of housing styles and gardens. Many neighborhoods with tree-lined streets sprang up around the commuter train stations.

"There can be few more attractive residential centers in this part of the world than Olivos, San Isidro, and San Fernando. All three of them lie along the low bluff that sets back a short distance from the low shore of the river, and from what might aptly be called the Westchester County of Buenos Aires," F. A. Sherwood observed in 1920.

Suburban life along the River Plate has managed to maintain much of the charm and the leisure that Westchester has lost to a certain extent since World War II. Porteños still have far more servants and more free time. As Rosita Forbes told readers in 1932: "In no other country in the world could one spend an afternoon sitting on a lawn in com-

ABOVE AND OPPOSITE

Imitation colonial tile, originally imported from France or Spain, gives a Spanish flavor to this convent built in the 1930s in the suburb of San Isidro. The rich design of the masonry is typical of that found on churches and palaces in seventeenth- and eighteenth-century colonial Latin America.

ABOVE *Fourteen columns grace the front of a home in the suburb of San Isidro. The columns' reflection in the formal pool underscores the symmetry of a European design imported to the edge of the pampa.*

LEFT *This magnificent property once commanded an unimpeded view of the River Plate. Now a number of neighbors intrude on the view from the swimming pool. Nevertheless, this well-situated estate is one of the prime ones remaining in San Isidro.*

RIGHT *What looks like a movie set awaiting the towel-draped body of a shapely film star is in reality the suburban bathroom of a sailboat designer and an interior decorator. This fantasy-fulfilling scene reflects the porteño's propensity for re-creating a Europe that even Europeans can't revive.*

LEFT *A sense of spaciousness, the cheering presence of sunlight, and a penchant for refined comfort combine to give this San Isidro living room the welcoming charm that still characterizes the porteño's attitude toward interior design.*

OPPOSITE *A seigneurial nineteenth-century mansion in San Isidro is a perfect example of how elegant country life around Buenos Aires must have been at the turn of the century. Tall pines offer shade and colorful jasmine bushes adorn the majestic gallery.*

This magnificent bay window protrudes from one of the grand salons at the Sans Souci Palace in the suburb of San Fernando. Designed by French architect René Sergent for the Alvear family, the stately mansion, with its well-kept gardens that once stretched to the river's edge, now caters to elegant weddings and other paid gatherings.

fortable basket chairs, old and young together, with half a dozen white-gloved menservants standing round doing nothing whatsoever. It was too early for tea, too late for any prolongation of lunch. There we sat, talking and laughing, and behind us, for no reason at all, were a host of liveried domestics. If somebody dropped a glove, it was discreetly retrieved. I think at one moment an extra ash-tray was brought from the house. New York has its tapestries and its gold plate taken from houses whose names made history in the Middle Ages, but New York is up against the servant problem. The butler has his own car and it is likely to be blocking the driveway when his master wants to go out in his roadster. But Argentina has, miraculously, retained or induced, in the middle of her vast productive plains, where the settler's life is raw as in the most primitive East, a feudalism unequalled today outside of the castles of royalist Hungary." Those select few who lived feudally in the 1930s no longer do so. But Argentina's social structure changes gradually, especially in the countryside.

"As to the 'homes' of the Argentine, they approach more nearly Anglo-Saxon ideas of 'comfort' than the French, Spanish, or Italian notions of 'home,'" wrote J. A. Hammerton in *The Real Argentina* back in 1915. "French styles of furniture and interior decoration still predominate. There is, however, a growing appreciation of the more solid comfort of English styles, and popularity for these is assured. Our capacious easy chairs are ousting the dainty, elegant and abominably unrestful French affairs. Little progress, however, has been made in the direction of heating the houses, and an Argentine interior in winter is apt to be a picture of shivering cheerlessness. But there are signs that even this will be remedied in the increasing approval of what may be described as English comfort. The drawing-room of most of the better-class homes is

LEFT *Sans Souci's stately columns face the nearby river and overlook a park that is planted with century-old trees. With dozens of bedrooms and enough service quarters to house a battalion, the palace was once the weekend home of the Alvear family and is still kept in perfect shape by its present owners.*

BELOW *The porte cochere of the Sans Souci Palace marks the elegant style of this masterpiece of French architecture transplanted to the River Plate.*

ABOVE *It could be mistaken for a lush park on the Loire River in France, but it is in fact Ivry, one of the many European-style estates in the suburbs and countryside surrounding Buenos Aires.*

RIGHT *The stately mansion is inspired by French country living in architecture, in landscaping, and even in name.*

ABOVE *Ivry is one of the few extant examples of the opulence that once characterized life at its best on the pampa. Every detail in the sumptuous dining room was meticulously transplanted from France.*

RIGHT *Except for a set of engravings of native birds, this tented bedroom looks authentically French Empire.*

BELOW *The gardens at Ivry, designed by French landscape architects, are especially spectacular in the autumn.*

LEFT *Even the intricate wrought-iron balustrade in Ivry's elaborate stairwell traveled by steamer across the Atlantic a century ago.*

BELOW *A whimsically elaborate wrought-iron rocking chair sits on tiles imported from Europe.*

Giant eucalyptus trees shield this weekend house in Pilar, a fast-growing residential area north of Buenos Aires, from both winter winds and summer sunlight. The wide gallery with its solid columns and the tiled roof are borrowed from traditional estancia architecture.

a gorgeously furnished chamber, in which the furniture, on most days of the year, is hidden under dust covers, and where blinds are seldom raised. It exists for state occasions only, when the starchiest formality is observed, and these are by no means numerous and always duly announced in the social column of the daily papers. The lady of the house passes most of her time between her bedroom and her boudoir, and it is in the latter, if she cultivates a circle of lady friends, that she will sip afternoon tea with her callers, although you will occasionally come across an announcement in the social news stating that some lady is going to give a 'five o'clock

tea room' at four o'clock, and inviting her acquaintances to be present. There is a great partiality for the use of English phrases, and 'five o'clock tea,' together with the addition of 'room,' is often used without any clear understanding of its meaning."

Life at a *quinta*, the equivalent of "a place in the country," reflects the idiosyncrasies of the owners, much more so than a downtown apartment or an estancia. Architectural styles are as varied as the nationalities of the owners' ancestors. The main difference today is the lack of security. Back in 1920, Sherwood complained, "As far as burglaries are concerned, I am entitled to speak feelingly, because

LEFT *Rustic elegance is characteristic of life in Pilar, the heart of horse country in the outlying suburbs. Distressed wooden beams, doors with large or small panes of glass, and shuttered windows are common features in old country homes.*

ABOVE *Pragmatic simplicity is the hallmark of a bathroom in this weekend home. The ceiling of tree branches is a typical feature of turn-of-the-century rural houses.*

LEFT *A roaring fire warms this patio, where a pot of steaming water waits for maté drinkers to gather around the fireplace. The simple natural wooden chairs are in keeping with the casual style of this weekend home in Pilar.*

RIGHT *During the hot summer months, many hours are spent in the shade of the gallery. A ceiling fan provides a breeze on windless days. The decor is rustic: a cowhide tablecloth, baskets, and comfortable rattanlike sofa and chairs.*

OPPOSITE *The towering mosquito net is reminiscent of colonial living in the tropics. This comfortable corner looks out on the weekend home's gardens.*

ABOVE *A motley collection of ceramic, glass, and silver objects provides the decorative focus of this dining room in Pilar. The split-pea green walls set off the whitewashed dado and give the room a fresh, festive air.*

LEFT *A seated Buddha is perhaps the only indication in this airy, informally decorated living room that the porteños who spend their weekends and summers at the edge of the pampa are also frequent fliers to both Europe and the Orient.*

RIGHT *The tile roof and rosy pink exterior give Alicia Goñi's country home a colonial flavor that is reinforced by the tile-covered gallery, the large ceramic jar set against a column, and the vines spreading out across the wall.*

ABOVE *A wicker basket of recently picked grapefruits on a decoratively painted wooden table creates a perfect still life to capture the color of country living in the suburbs near Buenos Aires.*

LEFT *Alicia Goñi's cat takes advantage of her owner's momentary absence to lap up the last few drops of her coffee. Soon Alicia will return to her reading and to the peace and harmony of her protected patio overlooking a park of uninterrupted greenery.*

RIGHT *The view of a walled garden from the sunken tub in this bathroom in Alicia Goñi's country home makes bathing a paradisiacal experience.*

ABOVE *The traditional charms of solid rustic furniture, natural wooden doors, a mirror reflecting a Botero poster, and a sideboard stained blue are whimsically offset by the lavender walls of the Mavroleon-Sly home.*

RIGHT *Bright colors and warm textures make this patio an inviting spot.*

OPPOSITE *The unexpected combines with the inventive at the suburban home of Alessandra Mavroleon and Richard Sly. Children's chairs are stored decoratively on the wall, complementing a pair of old lanterns suspended from the wooden staircase. Another chair, hooked over a supporting strut of a rustic table, adds to the quirkiness of the scene.*

thieves broke into our house at Olivos one night recently, and stole, among other things, every suit of clothes I possess. They even took the suit I had been wearing the evening before, and that was on a chair at the foot of the bed. In the morning I received the local Chief of Police in my pijamas, and was obliged to borrow clothes from a neighbor to enable me to get into town to buy others." Today, burglars usually take only electronic equipment, and the chief of police no longer makes house calls.

BELOW *The time-worn clubhouse of the Tigre Athletic Club, built at the turn of the century, remains a monument to the area's glorious past. The facade maintains its nobility, with wreaths and garlands adorning the arched doorways.*

RIGHT *The Tigre Club, designed by French architect Paul Pater, was inaugurated in 1906. The Prince of Wales, legendary tenor Enrico Caruso, and poet Ruben Dario were visitors in the club's heyday. Now the well-maintained building serves as Tigre's Municipal Cultural Center.*

Risks change with the times, and the day of carefree suburban living seems to have been replaced by a more restrictive lifestyle, within a self-contained "country." Many of the suburban streets have their own security guards stationed at sentry posts on strategic corners. In spite of the annoyance of such measures, suburban Buenos Aires is much safer than similar neighborhoods in São Paulo, where houses have turrets with machine-gun posts, or in Mexico City, where cars carry an armed guard in addition to the chauffeur.

Coveys of quintas and "countries" are tucked away along offshoots of the Paraná River, one of

The grand entrance and dock to the once spectacular Tigre Hotel is now a colonnaded curiosity, left to stir the imaginations of the nostalgic. Located near the juncture of the Lujan and Reconquista rivers, the hotel was destroyed by fire in 1944.

the major components of the River Plate, as they wiggle through what is probably the world's largest delta. The Tigre—the generic name given to the entire delta region—is a watery wonderland of small subtropical islets prone to flooding.

"It is a region of amazing beauty, which in its luxuriant vegetation, its myriad water ways, its charming summer homes, and its yacht and boat clubs, is a kind of rural Venice . . . aptly called by an English friend 'Green Heaven,'" observed United States Ambassador Alexander Weddell of the Tigre in his book *Introduction to Argentina* (1939).

Weddell also delved into the origin of the area's name: the Tiger. He came up with two versions. The first is the story of a man-eating *tigre* that savaged early settlers' cattle; in the second, a *tigre* was once spotted drifting down the river from Paraguay on a piece of floating riverbank.

The Tigre has had its dicey moments during the country's sporadic political upheavals, but no one has mentioned the presence of a dangerous feline since the Tigre Boat Club was founded in 1889, back when hundreds of Britishers spent weekends and summers in the island paradise.

Weddell gives us an overview of the architecture along the shores. "Charming villas, Swiss chalets, English cottages, Chinese pagodas, even Gothic cloisters, are to be seen, representing every architectural vagary one can imagine. Each property has its little landing stage where there is usually a bathing cabin, and often a sort of belvedere in which to sit and watch passers-by in the various river craft."

Until recently, adepts of the Tigre tended to be of a certain mentality: they had to have a high tolerance for mosquitoes, for instance, as well as a

As the sun sets, a boy and a man fish beneath the columns of the old Tigre Hotel entrance. No longer a playground for the well-to-do, the waterfront promenade now caters to locals.

ABOVE *A lacy hammock offers an inspiring view of the Tigre Delta from the porch of Christl von Plessen's home. The porch's columns are braced by handsomely curved wooden supports that highlight the building's fin de siècle air.*

RIGHT *This traditional Tigre home and its towering windmill are set on an island in the delta. A zinc-roofed gazebo greets guests on arrival. Built of oak and pinotea, the house was imported from England in 1904, as were many of the country homes around Buenos Aires.*

*One corner of the
wraparound porch makes
an ideal dining area on
summer days.*

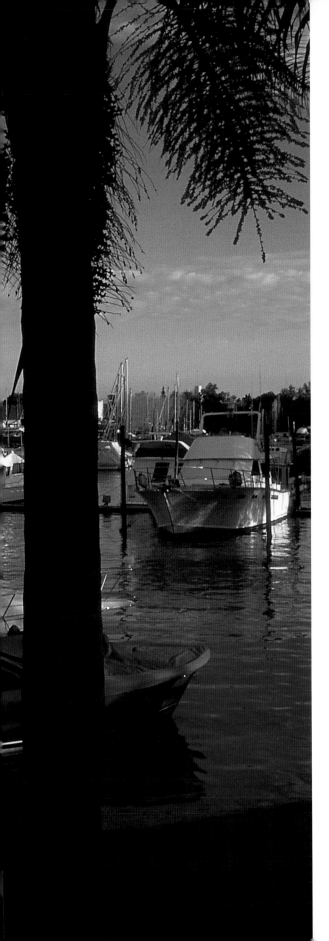

deep-seated need for solitude and a penchant for commuting by boat—whether their own, a taxi launch, or a floating *colectivo*, which stops at every inhabited inlet.

The Tigre has traditionally attracted people with a passion for fishing, boating, reading, eating and drinking, or loafing. Writers and artists, black sheep, and second-generation habitués comprise the hard-core population. Today the Tigre is undergoing a boom. Developers are building communities with marinas, new roads are providing quicker access, and Lynn University is duplicating its lake-dotted campus in Boca Raton, Florida.

ABOVE *A nautical service station on a river in Tigre where weekenders can fuel their motorboats. Regular passenger service on long, lean wooden vessels is available throughout the delta. There are numerous restaurants, several hotels, and vendors who ply the channels offering all sorts of merchandise.*

LEFT *The* Porteño *is one of many thousands of craft that weave through Tigre's intricate network of channels on weekends.*

FAR LEFT *Palm trees border the shoreline of the Argentine Yacht Club in San Fernando, a riverside suburb just south of Tigre. An international leader in sailboat design, greater Buenos Aires has one of the largest pleasure craft populations in the world.*

CHAPTER 5

The Countryside

Perhaps the only place where the country has managed to maintain much of its traditional character—its Argentineness—is at the estancia. The ranch remains its owner's domain; the ranch house, his castle. He shares the benefits of his fiefdom with no one except the taxman.

The Argentine countryside is called the "camp" by porteños. According to Reverend Currier, "The word *camp* has, clearly, been taken from the Spanish *campo,* the field or country, or, as they say in French, *la campagne.* The camp was originally divided up among the Spanish soldiers and those of their successors who were in a position to receive a grant from the Crown. These grants were vast tracts of pastureland measuring hundreds of square miles and pre-stocked with hundreds of thousands of wild cattle, the descendants of the animals brought down from Paraguay in an expedition led by Spanish conquistador Domingo de Irala in the sixteenth century.

Today's major estancias are the offshoots of these now legendary expanses that outstretched the largest spreads deep in the heart of Texas. Progress, estate laws, and taxes have provoked a steady change of hands: now American and European magnates and celebrities, such as Ted Turner and Jane Fonda, and George Soros, are buying

Motorcycles, cars, and pickup trucks have not yet completely replaced bicycles and horses as the primary means of transportation in the countryside around Buenos Aires.

TOP *Century-old trees dwarf a large estancia home near San Miguel del Monte. A carefully trimmed lawn provides a pleasing view for guests at teatime. Here, as in estates of similar style in Scarsdale or the Hamptons, graceful comfort is the key.*

BOTTOM *An estanciero flies in from Buenos Aires to check out how his favorite horses are doing. Most estancias have landing strips for small planes.*

up the most beautiful or the most productive ranches. But the tradition lingers on in many a corner of the pampa, and it is the magical world of the estancia—the rancher, the gaucho, the horse, the herds and flocks, the endless fields of ripening grain turning the landscape a delicate gold—that pervades the nature of the porteño. At a certain level of society, no self-respecting mother would allow her daughter to marry into a family without a significant estancia.

Dr. Franklin Martin, Director-General of the American College of Surgeons, describes his visit to a large estancia in 1922: "The hacienda consists of forty-five square miles of agricultural territory about halfway between Buenos Aires and La Plata [30 miles from Kilometer Zero]. This is one of the largest and most attractive landed estates in Argentina. . . . There are one hundred thousand cattle, two hundred thousand sheep, and other animals in proportion, and on which is raised quantities of grain, corn, and produce.

"The estancias are very much alike in construction, and vary only according to the resources of the owners. They are usually plain structures of wood and iron, and only occasionally do we find them built of brick. Those that boast a second story are few, though where the owner controls a large tract of territory and spends much of his time in personal supervision, we occasionally find a more ambitious effort in domestic architecture."

Dr. Martin apparently did not get to see other estancias and the wide variety of styles in which they are built. Now with safer roads, estancieros are spending more time on their estates, many of which have been brought up to date in terms of plumbing, heating, and lighting.

Ambassador Weddell describes his visit to an estancia near Tandil: "The beautiful modern home, built in the Spanish style, is set in the midst of a park which is reached from the gate of the estancia by an avenue formed of poplars *(Populus canadensis)* over six miles long."

At nearby Acelain, one of the classic estancias, Weddell was struck by "the great house, furnished with old world treasures, with chapel, cloister, guest-wing and beautiful Spanish gardens, whose long pools and cool greens vied with the blaze of color of the other and flower-planted gardens." On another day Weddell described his impressions of Villa María, close to Buenos Aires. "The gracious, rambling house, with deep verandas, is set in an extensive park with fine trees. I remember stately processions of pedigreed bulls being led across the foot of the lawn for inspection by the guests, the great animals with gentle eyes, waddling on their peg-like legs, seemingly quite aware of their perfection."

The perfect, peg-legged, pedigreed bulls are as self-aware as ever, but most, like the estancieros themselves, have moved farther into the countryside, as ranch land near the city is now being turned into industrial parks or country-club compounds. Livestock in the pampa graze the range. The flavor and texture of a range-fed steer is impossible to duplicate, and that is why Argentine steaks are so famous.

More and more ranchers are diversifying into stocking deer for foreign hunters to shoot; some are even experimenting with the New Zealand deer that are raised for their meat in closed fields with very high fences. Rabbit and pheasant stocks have been greatly depleted since the beginning of the century. And dove shooting attracts hunters from abroad, most of whom return home delighted with their results.

The estancia today is part myth, part reality. Like so many facets of porteño life, the form may seem the same, but the content has changed. The acreage, or square mileage, of the major estancias

has shrunk, as have the comforts of a once stately lifestyle. Many of the grand homes are now, like everywhere in the world, upscale inns, offering the affluent traveler a glimpse into camp life and tradition before it lost its splendor.

In any case, it must never be forgotten that estancias produce a major portion of Argentina's wealth, in exports as well as feeding the thirty-three million inhabitants of the country. The lifestyle may have lost its dazzle, but productivity remains on the rise, guaranteeing Argentina a sound economic future.

No matter what happens in real terms, the folkloric image of the Argentine pampas remains intact. The stock image of the camp is that of a white-bearded gaucho sitting under an ombú

ABOVE *A master* asador, *who has worked at the late Carlos Miguens's estancia, El Rosario, for more than thirty years, slices a perfectly grilled chunk of rare steak. The secret is to grill the meat gradually over no-longer-red embers.*

LEFT *One of Carlos Miguens's passions was bullfights. A political exile in Spain for five years, he befriended most of the top toreadors and returned with his trophies: the head of a Mihura bull killed by Jaime Ostós and posters of corridas he witnessed.*

RIGHT *An abandoned thatched gazebo stands at the edge of El Rosario on the marshy shores of Laguna de Monte, a large lake that also borders the nearby town of San Miguel del Monte. Over the years this shady spot has been the site of picnics, drinks after fishing, tea before boating, and relaxation after a ride on horseback or a hike.*

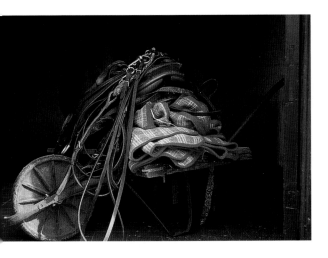

LEFT *A vintage wheelbarrow provides a home for a variety of riding gear, ready for the use of weekend polo players and other equestrians.*

BELOW *El Rosario was built more than a century ago by a Spanish officer from Málaga. At the time the nearby town of San Miguel del Monte was a fortress erected to protect the pampas from marauding bands of Indians.*

ABOVE *Carlos Miguens at El Rosario, in August 1998. Beloved by all who knew him, he was a magnet for young and old throughout his life.*

ABOVE *The stately facade of Benquerencia, one of the most handsome estancia homes, is set in the midst of a carefully groomed park. The vast Argentine pampa is dotted with magnificent mansions of many different styles, including precise replicas of French châteaux.*

LEFT *The* padrillera, *or stable for* padrillos—*the productive stallions of the pampas—was designed in colonial style, as were many of Benquerencia's buildings.*

RIGHT *The fifteen-foot ceiling in this handsomely tiled bathroom at Benquerencia helps keep the temperature tolerable, even at the height of summer.*

ABOVE *Tiles set in geometrical patterns, wrought-iron grillwork, and an intricately carved and polychromed mantelpiece at Benquerencia provide a Spanish backdrop for colonial religious wood carvings.*

RIGHT *A set of golf clubs stands in stark contrast to the traditional Spanish colonial decor of a bedroom at Benquerencia. A woven poncho from northern Argentina is stretched out on the elaborately carved bed.*

RIGHT *A blazing fire adds a touch of warmth to the living room designed by Luisa Miguens and Emilia Serantes for hotel owner Junichi Iwasaki, the first Japanese convert to polo. Located in Pilar, Iwasaki's home is a horse farm that once was a way station for Haras "Comalal," one of Argentina's most important thoroughbred operations.*

BELOW *A stall that once housed a thoroughbred champion now is the stage for tango-singing gauchos. Rodrigo Rueda, the host, offers his guests maté and empanadas along with the melancholic music. A gigantic fogón can be used when the weather is too inclement to grill outdoors.*

sipping maté. Each of these three components has a special meaning for the porteño. Combined, they represent all that is noble and enduring in camp mythology.

The gaucho has been glorified in the movies, dissected by sociologists, and immortalized in literature. Christopher Isherwood captures his essence in *The Condor and the Cows* (1949). "The original type of Gaucho—the homeless horseman, the knife-fighter, the romantic wanderer of the plains—is as extinct as the cowboy of the Old West. But his legend—like that of the cowboy in our western movies—is very much alive. It is classically preserved in the epic poem *Martín Fierro*, Argentina's national Iliad, from which most people can quote at least a few passages. And probably the gaucho legend has something to do with that excessive

LEFT *The stately stables at Clio-Hué are part of an old estancia that has been converted into a country inn where guests are offered polo lessons as well as the best of domesticated gaucho living. A farmhand, dressed in gaucho finery, leads a polo pony out to exercise.*

ABOVE *Rodrigo Rueda, Junichi Iwasaki's best friend in Argentina, manager of his horse farm, and on-the-spot host to his guests, carries an antler-handled* facón *(knife) in his silver belt, which he wears atop a colorful hand-woven band.*

cult of *Machismo,* Maleness or Virility, which still flourishes here, even among the city-dwellers of Buenos Aires."

Most people's awareness of Argentine-style machismo derives from Hollywood and the likes of Rudolph Valentino. In recent years, the role of women has been given much press in Buenos Aires, and being excessively macho is no longer tolerated by the society, even though many women, especially mothers, still encourage the attitude in the males under their influence. There still are numerous macho gauchos roaming the plains, but little by little they are being domesticated.

Juan José Güiraldes, the nephew of the author of Argentina's other gaucho classic, *Don Segundo Sombra* (1926), and president of the Confederación Gaucha Argentina, declares, "Today's gaucho is dark, or blond and blue-eyed. He may be a mix of Yugoslavian and Irish, Irish and Spanish, or Spanish and Scottish. . . . This mix occurred in only two countries of the world: in the United States and in Argentina. However, the American cowboy appeared in the last century, while the Argentine gaucho dates back to the seventeenth century."

Seventeenth-century gauchos were a rough and tumble breed, a mix of swarthy Spanish foot soldiers and primitive Indian women. The first-generation gaucho spent too much time trying to stay alive to be able to be considered romantic. He was a survivor, a nomadic outsider, whose progeny, after several generations, began to mix with immigrants and natives alike, finally becoming the colorful character of late-nineteenth-century lore.

Taking a look at his origins, George Pendle writes in *Argentina* (1955), "Historically the gaucho was unhappy in his origin and in his fate. The word *gaucho* is probably of Quechuan Indian derivation and signifies an orphan, a lost soul. The gaucho was originally the offspring of the Spanish invader

and the Indian woman, whom the Spaniard subjugated but rarely married. There, as Carlos Octavio Bunge wrote, he was from birth 'an orphan of civilization.' But this nomadic horseman had his revenge on 'civilization': he communicated the sadness of the desolate pampa, and of his own experience, to the inhabitants of the city; and the melancholy of his *tristes,* or laments, accompanied on the guitar, was echoed in urban tangos, whose verses almost invariably expressed disillusion and frustration."

In 1865 a British observer, Thomas J. Hutchinson, wrote in his book *Buenos Ayres and Argentine Gleanings* (as cited by Pendle), "Set a Gaucho to dance, and he moves as if he were on a procession to his execution; ask him to sing, and he gives utterance to sounds resembling an Irish keen, accompanied by nasal drones suggestive of croup; put him to play the guitar, and you feel your flesh beginning to creep, for the tinkling elicited is as if a number of sick crickets were crackling their legs over the fingers of the player."

Hutchinson's colorful comments no longer hold true. Today gauchos are more melodic and less morose, more rhythmic and less mournful. But still, "Home on the Range" will never be a model for the gaucho's taste in music.

In *The Amazing Argentine* (1910), John Foster Fraser gives a useful overview of the gaucho's place in rural Argentine history. "The most characteristic figure of the camp town is the gaucho. He is the native of the plains, and is usually of mixed blood. The idle, independent, nomad gauchos are almost an extinct class. In the early days they refused to settle anywhere, or do any regular work. They were horsemen and hunters, and roamed over the plains, staying here and there in ramshackle huts till restlessness, or the owner of the land, moved them on. They were the gypsies of Argentina. Whenever there was a war or a revolution the gaucho would

OPPOSITE, LEFT *An antique facón with a silver handle and sheath, placed within easy reach, is tucked in this gaucho's rastra (belt), which is elegantly adorned with a series of starlike flowers set in circles and the owner's initials, all crafted in silver.*

OPPOSITE, RIGHT *This elegant young gaucho in his most formal attire is in fact typical of the gauchos at any country fair in Argentina. Black hat, black poncho with a geometric indigenous pattern, leather crop, hand-woven native saddle blanket, and silver stirrups comprise the rider's accoutrements.*

be found in the vanguard, and in times of peace he would enliven the dullness with private feuds which did not end with words."

Fraser adds, "But civilisation has been too strong for him, and the modern gaucho is a more law-abiding and useful person. He still wears his old, picturesque costume, the broad sombrero, the shirt, the wide Turkish trousers, which may be of any color in the spectrum, tucked into his boots. In cold weather he wears over his shoulder the poncho, a blanket which has as many varieties of hue as his trousers. His saddle is ornamented with silver, and he has fancy stirrups and jingling spurs. But the chief part of his equipment is the big knife —often a foot long and usually of fancy pattern— stuck in his belt. This is used freely for defensive purposes, or to avenge some real or imaginary insult; it also serves when eating his lunch."

Inveterate horsemen, gauchos of old never dismounted, eating and often sleeping atop their mounts when on the road. As the saying goes, the oneness of the gaucho and his horse is as intimate as the clenched couple executing the complex glides of the tango. The gaucho and the tango dancer are crucial to comprehending what makes porteños tick.

ABOVE *Carts driven by gauchos dressed in their Sunday best compete at La Rural, the annual country fair held right in the center of Buenos Aires. The horses are surprisingly agile for their size, maneuvering around obstacles with the elan of polo ponies.*

RIGHT *A saddleless rider, mounted atop a* recado *(a sheepskin and a leather blanket), a* rebenque *(rawhide whip) at his side, sports* potro *boots (made from the hide of the leg of a young horse), a hand-woven band to hold them up, and a pair of antique silver stirrups.*

ABOVE *The camera closes in to capture post–gaucho chic: finely stitched natural leather boots, decoratively pleated white cotton* bombachas *(riding pants), and braided rawhide suspenders, set against the rich blue body and textured floor paneling of a rural utility vehicle.*

❧

Maté is an infusion that the people of the River Plate drink day in and day out. In both the city and the camp, one sees men with a thermos tucked under one arm, and a maté and a *bombilla*, or long straw, held in the other hand. The ritual of the maté is vital for a significant portion of the people on the pampa, whether they are driving, on horseback, or lounging in a chair watching the world go by.

"I must tell you something about *yerba mate*, the national drink of South America," Delight Prentiss told her readers in 1905, "for I have grown very fond of it, and the after effect seems harmless. The yerba is a low-growing bush, and the mate is made from its dried leaves and twigs, a discovery of the Jesuit missionaries, it is said. In serving it there is just one small gourd (mate) or silver cup used for a whole family group, successive fillings with hot water only improving the flavor, the decoction being sipped slowly through a long tube called a *bombilla*, having an end with holes in it. After the boiling water is first poured on the powdered yerba, the cup is passed to the most important person present or to the honored guest; then after a sip it goes on from one to another, the gourd being filled up with boiling water as required, and sometimes another pinch of fresh yerba added. So it goes on its round again and again, no one ever expecting to get his fill at any one time. The taste is not unpleasant even at first; something between licorice, cocoa, and Garfield tea, and I can't help thinking they get the material for the latter from down here, yerba being very cheap.'"

Nothing has changed in the way yerba is imbibed in the century since Prentiss's description. Some people add sugar, but that is frowned upon by the serious maté drinker. It can also be served cold in summer, like iced tea, and can be found bottled like a soft drink, but these too are distortions of the true ceremony, and no genuine gaucho will ever be caught indulging in such sacrilege.

The banged-up, blackened kettle, busily boiling over a bristling fire, a battered tin can brimming with yerba, and a gaucho with a rustic gourd, often incised or engraved with a design, and a bombilla of silver or cheap metal, according to his status and prosperity, clutched in his knotted fingers is a scene as native to the landscape as the horse and the ombú.

The final image of our rural trinity is the ombú. A bizarre configuration of expanding roots and

Maté drinking at its most refined: sipped through a silver bombilla from a gourd nestled in a finely crafted silver holder.

spreading branches, this would-be tree has been immortalized in the paintings of Uruguayan artist Pedro Figari and Argentine Nicolás García Uriburu. *Ombú* in guaraní means "shades," and offering respite from the sun has been its principal function. According to Pendle, "The lonely, indigenous tree of the pampa, the ombú, has become almost a national emblem. The ombú is known as the lighthouse of the pampa, because (until groves of fast-growing eucalyptus trees were planted around the occasional estancia houses) it was the only object to be seen on the sea-like plains. It has an enormous trunk and its widely-spreading branches cover a large space of ground, while its knotted roots, protruding above the surface of the land, offer a convenient resting-place to weary horsemen. The ombú lives for innumerable years: no cyclone can blow it down, nor can fire destroy it; and its pulpy wood is useless to man even as fuel. Thus although it is a friendly tree for the rider and his mount when the sun is high, the ombú in reality is a lonely weed, a fit symbol of Argentina's solitude."

The ombú, which could spread like bamboo; yerba maté, a tea able to provide sustenance and solace to the solitary gaucho; and the gaucho himself, nomadic and romantic, evoke a much more intense and dramatic image than the cactus, coffee, and cowboy of American folklore. Porteños owe their comfortable existence to the pampa as much as to the port. Both have been fundamental in forging their personality and their values, just as their vision of history tempers their expectations for the future.

In *South of Us* (1930), writer and critic Waldo Frank elegizes Buenos Aires in a poetic riff. "Boulevards of showy breadth, hippodromes, plazas, parkways with intricate embroidery of flowers, and melting

the ostentation, the same softness, ripe and remote —an air so subtly real that it mellows the marble, warms the gait of worldly men, widens the eyes of women."

The porteños, at home at the end of the line, blessed with a brilliant sun, ensconced in an aura of light that, at dawn or dusk, can still the tremors of the soul, are but outcasts of a distant world, proud of pasts heralded and unheralded, and yet preoccupied at their very core with what awaits them after the ultimate separation from Europe.

Buenos Aires, a city that houses so many, seems like home to so few. The porteño thrives on migrating in his imagination, romantically transplanting himself to what he expects to be a more prosperous land, like the Argentina that his ancestors were once promised when they signed up for the transatlantic passage. Romantically, a more pastoral setting lures him; pragmatically, a higher level of infrastructure; and culturally, a yearning to be where the action is.

In any attempt to evaluate Argentina and the Argentines, it is vital to take a second glimpse. The surface is often deceiving, because so much about life in Buenos Aires is superficial. But beneath that now tarnished skin of the biggest, the best, and the longest, a vitality burns that yearns for the promise of the future.

There is, of course, another Buenos Aires, one that is, like the tide, carrying the city into the new millennium, one that will be a meaty theme for future visitors and chroniclers. In the meantime, Buenos Aires is what it is today—a city that carries its past on its lapel like a miniature flag, a warm heart beating beneath.

The tango seems to contain the core of the city's lament. "The ritual celebration of nostalgia is now in itself part of the country's nostalgia for its vanished glories," author Pico Iyer comments in

Falling off the Map (1993). Buenos Aires, however, is not just a wistful has-been, in spite of the tango's lyrics of regret and twang of sorrow. In its long-standing crusade to recuperate the irretrievable "best in the world" status in so many categories, Buenos Aires, like many of its more intellectually oriented citizens, seems to depend on the process of recall to satisfy its search for the substance of the present. Out of the agonizing practice of self-investigation, porteños may be able to put their celerity and vitality into carving out a more fruitful future—a future truer to their unique heritage.

Visitor's Guide

Museums

Casa de Yrurtia
O'Higgins 2390
Belgrano
Tel.: 4-781-0385
The house and workshop of Rogelio Yrurtia (1879–1950), the sculptor responsible for the main monuments of Buenos Aires. Designed in the best Spanish baroque style, the museum features an amazing secret garden.

Museo de Arte Español "Enrique Larreta"
Juramento 2291
Belgrano
Tel.: 4-783-2640/4-784-4040
A few blocks from the Casa de Yrurtia is the Museo de Arte Español "Enrique Larreta" (Enrique Larreta Museum of Spanish Art), which specializes in Spanish art of the eighteenth to twentieth centuries. It is installed in a nineteenth-century building that was once the home of Enrique Larreta, author of the historical novel Don Ramiro's Glory. *The museum overlooks an Andalusian-style garden, complete with Moorish fountains, that is unique in Buenos Aires.*

Museo de Arte Hispanoamericano "Isaac Fernández Blanco"
Suipacha 1422
Barrio Norte
Tel.: 4-327-0272/4-327-0228
The Museo de Arte Hispano-americano "Isaac Fernández Blanco" (Isaac Fernández Blanco Museum of Spanish-American Art) was Isaac Fernández Blanco's donation to the Municipality of Buenos Aires in 1922. In 1936 the museum was relocated to its present site, a stately home that once belonged to architect Martín Noel. Built in the Neocolonial style, it is characteristic of the architecture of the 1920s; its gardens are of Spanish inspiration. The museum holds one of the most important collections in the Americas of colonial silver objects from Upper Peru. It also features a collection of paintings from the schools of Cuzco, Upper Peru and Argentina; Jesuitical imagery; carved imagery; furniture; high hair combs; porcelain; fans; and decorative arts of the republican period.

Museo de Arte Moderno
San Juan 350
San Telmo
Tel.: 4-361-3953/4-361-1121
The Museo de Arte Moderno (Museum of Modern Art) is located in an old tobacco warehouse in the traditional neighborhood of San Telmo. It houses its own collection—a wealth of concrete art, art informel, *and neofigurative art by Argentine painters and sculptors—as well as works by renowned foreign painters and sculptors.*

Museo de Artes Plásticas "Eduardo Sívori"
Av. Infanta Isabel 555
Palermo
Tel.: 4-774-9452/4-774-3855
The Museo de Artes Plásticas "Eduardo Sívori" (Eduardo Sívori Museum of Plastic Arts) makes its home in a recently renovated building overlooking the paseo del Rosedal in Palermo. It has a large collection of the best Argentine artists and now organizes special exhibits.

Museo de la Ciudad
Alsina 412
Centro
Tel.: 4-331-9855/4-343-2123
The Museo de la Ciudad (Museum of the City) occupies the first floor of the Farmacia de la Estrella, a house built in 1894 in the historical part of Buenos Aires near the Casa Rosada.

Its artifacts and exhibits truly reflect the "memory of the city."

MUSEO HISTÓRICO NACIONAL
Defensa 1600
San Telmo
Tel.: 4-307-1182/4-307-4457

The Museo Histórico Nacional (National Historical Museum) was founded on May 24, 1889, for the purpose of commemorating the period comprising the May Revolution and the wars of independence. It occupies a large old house that has recently undergone complete restoration and is one of the most genuine specimens of stately mid-nineteenth-century architecture. It is located in Lezama Square, on the site where Pedro de Mendoza is said to have founded Buenos Aires in 1536.

MUSEO DE MOTIVOS POPULARES ARGENTINOS "JOSÉ HERNÁNDEZ"
Av. del Libertador 2373
Palermo
Tel.: 4-802-7294/4-803-2384

The Museo de Motivos Populares Argentinos "José Hernández" (José Hernández Museum of Argentine Popular Subjects) holds one of the most important and complete collections of traditional Argentine crafts, including native silverwork and outstanding pieces made of leather, horn, wood, and iron. Among the objects are fancy gaucho buckles, tinderboxes, horse trappings, a wide variety of stirrups, and a magnificent collection of silver matés. The life-size reproduction of a pulpería (rural Spanish-American grocery store and drinking establishment) evokes daily life in the nine-teenth-century Buenos Aires countryside.

MUSEO NACIONAL DE ARTE DECORATIVO
Av. del Libertador 1902
Palermo
Tel.: 4-806-8306/4-801-8248

The Museo Nacional de Arte Decorativo (National Museum of Decorative Art) is located in one of the most beautiful buildings in the city. A typical example of the architecture found in Buenos Aires at the beginning of the century, it was designed by René Sergent before World War I. He was commissioned by Matías Errázuriz, the husband of Josefina de Alvear.

MUSEO NACIONAL DE ARTE ORIENTAL
Av. del Libertador 1902, piso 1
Palermo
Tel.: 4-801-5988

The upper floor of the Errázuriz palace has harbored the Museo Nacional de Arte Oriental (Museum of Oriental Art) since August 5, 1966. Devoted to Asian, African, and Oceanic cultures, the museum offers pieces of superb craftsmanship and great artistic value. The future home of the museum's valuable collection is currently being restored.

MUSEO NACIONAL DE BELLAS ARTES
Av. del Libertador 1473
Recoleta
Tel.: 4-803-8814/4-803-4691

The Museo Nacional de Bellas Artes (National Museum of Fine Arts), one of the major muse-ums of its kind in the Americas, was founded on July 16, 1895. In 1910 it was relocated to the Argentine Pavilion overlooking Plaza San Martín. Finally, in 1931 it was transferred to the buildings of the original Casa de Bombas de Aguas Corrientes in Recoleta, which were remodeled and adapted by architect Alejandro Bustillo. It has thirty-two halls on three floors, two patios for the exhibition of sculptures, a library, an audio-visual room, and restoration workshops.

MUSEO XUL SOLAR
Laprida 1212
Recoleta
Tel.: 4-824-3302

The Museo Xul Solar (Xul Solar Museum) operates in what used to be Xul Solar's (1887–1963) home. The artist himself had requested that his house be transformed into a center for cultural events imbued with a "club" spirit. It does indeed reflect his idea that a museum should be a meeting place for artists, thinkers, and people interested in art and science.

Cultural Centers and Galleries

BRITISH ARTS CENTER
Suipacha 1333
Centro
Tel.: 4-393-6941

CENTRO CULTURAL BORGES
San Martin 760
Centro
Tel.: 4-319-5359

CENTRO CULTURAL FUNDACIÓN
PROA
Av. Pedro de Mendoza 1929
La Boca
Tel.: 4-303-0909

CENTRO CULTURAL GENERAL
SAN MARTÍN
Av. Corrientes 1551
Centro
Tel.: 4-374-1251

CENTRO CULTURAL RECOLETA
Junín 1930
Recoleta
Tel.: 4-803-1041

CENTRO CULTURAL ROJAS
Av. Corrientes 2038
Centro
Tel.: 4-954-5521

All of the galleries listed below specialize in
contemporary Argentine art.

GALERÍA ART HOUSE
Uruguay 1223 casa 9
Barrio Norte

GALERÍA ARTE X ARTE
Vuelta de Obligado 2080, 3rd floor
Belgrano
Tel.: 4-788-3721

GALERÍA ATICA
Libertad 1240, 1st floor, Apt. 9
Tel.: 4-813-3544

GALERÍA FUNDACIÓN FEDERICO
KLEMM
M. T. de Alvear 626/8
Retiro
Tel.: 4-311-2527

GALERÍA NIKO GULLANDT
Bulnes 2241, 1st floor, Apt. B
Palermo
Tel.: 4-822-2064

GALERÍA NEXUS
Suipacha 1151
Retiro
Tel.: 4-393-9638

GALERÍA PALATINA
Arroyo 821
Retiro
Tel.: 4-327-0620

GALERÍA PRAXIS
Arenales 1311
Recoleta
Tel.: 4-813-8639

GALERÍA RUBBERS
Suipacha 1175
Retiro
Tel.: 4-393-6010

GALERÍA RUTH BENZACAR
Florida 1000
Retiro
Tel.: 4-313-8480

GALERÍA SARA GARCÍA URIBURU
Uruguay 1223
Recoleta
Tel.: 4-813-0148

GALERÍA VAN EYCK
Av. Santa Fe 834
Retiro
Tel.: 4-311-6568

GALERÍA VAN RIEL
Talcahuano 1257
Barrio Norte
Tel.: 4-811-8359

GALERÍA VYP
Arroyo 959
Retiro
Tel.: 4-325-8175

Theaters

AVENIDA
Av. de Mayo 1222
Tel.: 4-381-0662
Drama, concerts

BLANCA PODESTA
Av. Corrientes 1283
Tel.: 4-382-7652
Drama

CERVANTES
Libertad 815
Tel.: 4-816-4224
Drama, concerts

COLÓN
Libertad 621
Tel.: 4-382-5414
Opera, ballet, concerts

DEL SUR
Venezuela 1286
Tel.: 4-383-5702
Drama

GENERAL SAN MARTÍN
Av. Corrientes 1530
Tel.: 4-371-0111
Drama, concerts

GRAND REX
Av. Corrientes 857
Tel.: 4-322-8000
Movie theater, concert hall

LICEO
Av. Rivadavia 1499
Tel.: 4-381-4291
Drama

MAIPO
Esmeralda 433
Tel.: 4-322-4882
Revues, drama

MARGARITA XIRGU
Chacabuco 875
Tel.: 4-300-2448
Rock and traditional music concerts, drama

OPERA
Av. Corrientes 860
Tel.: 4-326-1335
Movie theater, rock concerts, musicals

PRESIDENTE ALVEAR
Av. Corrientes 1659
Tel.: 4-374-6076
Drama, concerts

Restaurants

CABAÑAS LAS LILAS
Av. A. M. de Justo 516
Puerto Madero
Tel.: 4-313-1336
Cabañas Las Lilas offers export-grade beef in any form desired, plus all the steer's innards grilled to perfection. If you like your steak rare, insist, because local palates prefer their meat on the gray side. Located in Puerto Madero, a waterfront view is part of the pleasure.

CATALINAS
Reconquista 875
Retiro
Tel.: 4-313-8430
Catalinas has maintained a tradition of preferring perfection to posturing. Chef Ramiro is a Spaniard who knows what his faithful clientele deserve. A carefully constructed decor adds to the delight of a wonderful meal from one of the top half-dozen kitchens in the city.

CLARK'S
Junín 1777
Recoleta
Tel.: 4-801-9502
Clark's is a traditional meeting place for businessmen, diplomats, and the like. Started by the city's most high-profile chef, Gato Dumas, the menu still bears traces of his eclectic imagination.

CLARK'S SARMIENTO
Sarmiento 645
Centro
Tel.: 4-325-1960
Clark's Sarmiento is the downtown version of the Recoleta Clark's. Set amid the shiny wooden fittings of what was once the city's most elegant men's haberdashery, solid meals are served—usually to businessfolk at midday—in a relaxing Old World atmosphere. Meat is often the best choice.

CLUB SIRIO LIBANÉS
Pacheco de Melo 1900
Recoleta
Tel.: 4-806-5764
Club Sirio Libanés is an ethnic nook where the Near Eastness of Buenos Aires comes to the fore. Excellent Lebanese meals in an old home in Recoleta redecorated to echo the East give the visitor a chance to recognize the relevance of the Syrio-Lebanese community in the city.

DORÁ
Av. Leandro N. Alem 1016
Retiro
Tel.: 4-311-2891
Dorá is the Real Thing: a no-frills, noisy, busy eatery where the accent is on quality and quantity, and the clients expect nothing but the best in straightforward food. The portions are enormous and the local version of a doggy bag is supplied to those who decide to finish their delicious steak or salmon at home.

EL CORRALÓN
Anchorena 916
Barrio Norte
tel.: 4-963-0838
El Corralón is a friendly, publike restaurant located between Barrio Norte and Palermo. Families, friends, and neighbors gather to talk as well as eat. El Corralón provides a taste of what the average restaurant-going porteño eats on a normal night out.